The Connoisseur
con·nois·seur | /ˌkanəˈsər"/
noun

- One who possesses expert knowledge and refined appreciation of the finer things; a judge of quality and excellence.

- A person whose passion for collecting transcends mere acquisition—who understands provenance, craftsmanship, and the stories behind exceptional objects.

- Someone who knows the difference between owning and understanding; between having everything and knowing what matters.

The Connoisseur is a twice-yearly publication for those who have moved beyond the surface of luxury into its deeper currents. Published each December and June, we explore the worlds of art, horology, automotive excellence, fine wines, and craftsmanship with the depth and sophistication our readers demand.

It is a publication for those who understand that true connoisseurship is earned through knowledge, experience, and passion—never simply purchased.

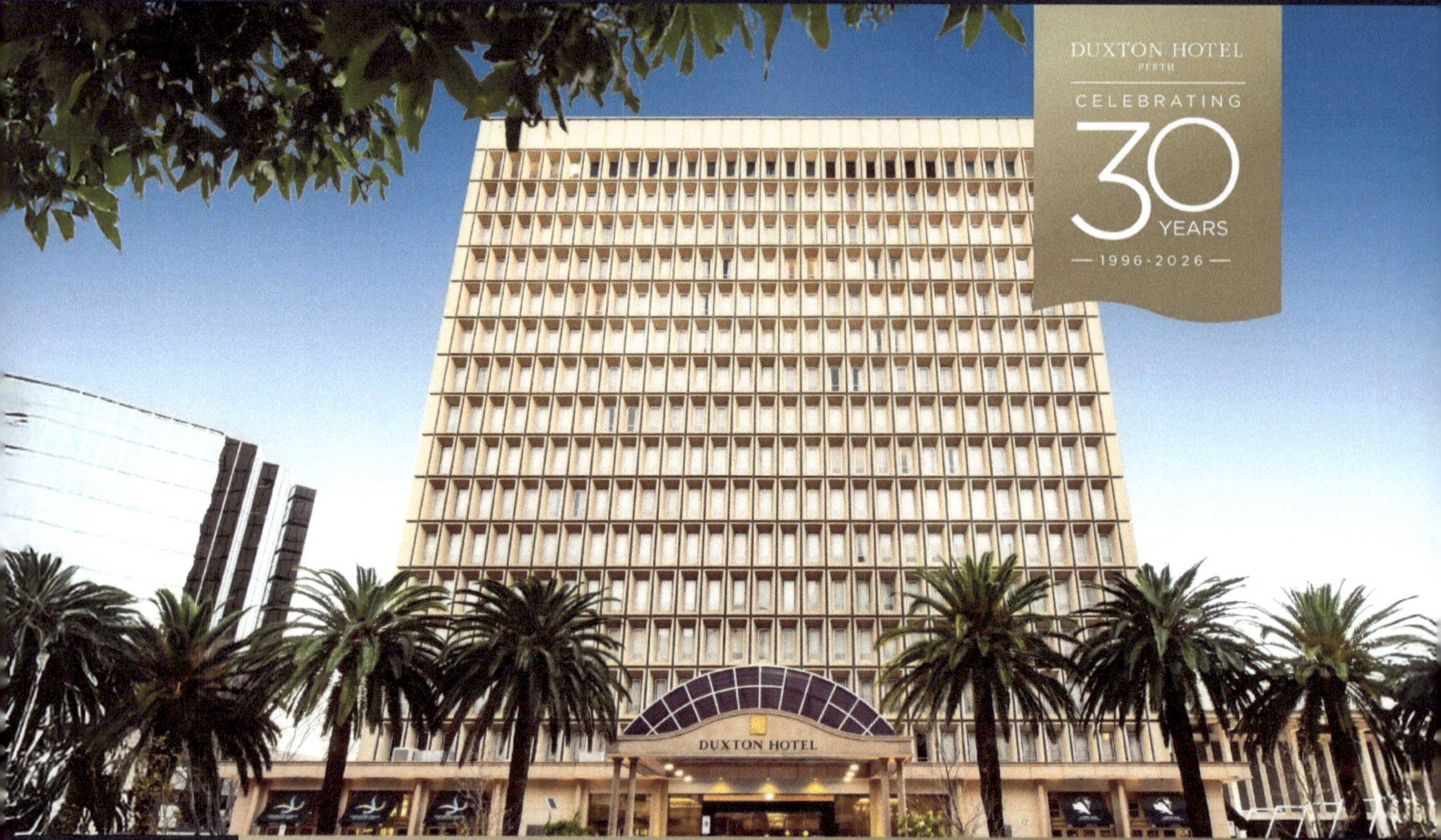

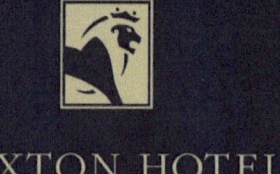

Distinctly Duxton

Discover luxury redefined at Duxton Hotel Perth, a 5-star gem in the heart of the Central Business District. Thoughtfully designed to blend contemporary sophistication with classic elegance, the hotel offers an elevated experience for both business and leisure guests. Where timeless heritage meets modern luxury.

DUXTON HOTEL
PERTH

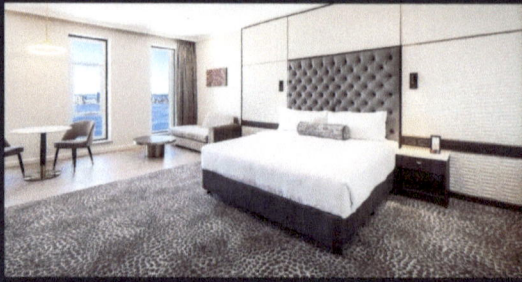

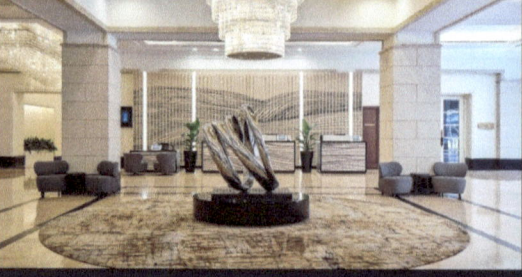

For inquiries and reservations:
T: (08) 9261 8000 | Reservations: 1800 681 118

Follow us:
duxtonhotelperth

E: reservations@perth.duxton.com.au

www.perth.duxtonhotels.com

Contents

Summer / Autumn 2026

The Brief

12 | *Death of the Impulse Purchase*
Why the most sophisticated collectors are spending more time researching and less time buying.

14 | *Wine Investing for Beginners: Don't*
A contrarian take: why buying wine to drink (not flip) makes you a better collector and a happier person.

17 | *In Defence of the Copy*
When is an homage acceptable, and when does it cross into theft? A nuanced look at inspiration, appropriation, and the murky ethics of design borrowing.

24 | *The Quiet Revolution in Hotel Luxury*
Why the world's most discerning travellers are abandoning mega-resorts for intimate properties with 10 rooms or less.

New Discoveries

28 | *When Yolŋu Art Becomes High Fashion*
Bula'bula Arts Centre x Black Cat Couture: A groundbreaking fashion collaboration brings Yolŋu art to the runway.

30 | *The High-Beat Pioneer Returns*
Longines Ultra-Chron Classic: A meticulously faithful revival of a 1967 high-beat icon that reminds us why Longines matters.

32 | *Where River Grapes Meet Coastal Botanicals*
Wise Gin: Margaret River's coastal spirit captures the essence of Western Australia in every small-batch bottle.

IMAGES: Opposite: The 2026 INVICTVS Range, Courtesy Buratti Collezione | Top: A private yacht charter in the Mediterrean. Courtesy StockCake | Below: Longines Ultra Chrona Automatic watch. Courtesy Longines.

Luxury Intelligence

34 | *Luxury Market Intelligence*
Art Basel Miami kicks off December, Japanese whisky is up 80%, Hermès Birkins trade at triple retail and the 1990s Porsche market has gone mad.

46 | *Collecting the Uncollectable*
The Rise of Experience-Based Luxury: Ultra-wealthy individuals are abandoning traditional luxury goods for exclusive experiences that money can barely buy.

52 | *Why Fashion Has Become the Investment You Can Wear*
Certain designer pieces have demonstrated remarkable appreciation, with Dior and Prada resale values increasing by 12% and 11% respectively. The emergence of fashion as a recognised artistic discipline worthy of serious collecting.

58 | *TAG Heuer's Best Kept Secret*
The watch brand's longest-running model defined a generation of tool-watch collecting.

62 | *The Case against Compromise*
A 60-kilogram weight reduction and the most powerful rear-drive Ferrari ever made.

Feature

68 | *The Price of Admission*
What it actually costs to become a serious collector in watches, wine, art, and cars—including the hidden expenses nobody tells you about.

The Makers

80 | *The Luminous Landscapes of Tim Storrier*
An exploration of one of Australia's most celebrated artists and his enduring fascination with the Australian landscape.

88 | *The Art of Not Taking Yourself Too Seriously*
Three industry veterans abandon convention to champion Margaret River's overlooked vineyards and the results are anything but goon.

The Grand Tour

92 | *Breaking New Ground*
Melbourne Art Fair's bold gamble on Design: How the fair is evolving to embrace design as a collecting category.

96 | *Concrete Ambitions*
Brutalism's Unlikely Luxury Masterpiece: Why the architectural style once derided is now commanding premium prices.

Collector Classic

104 | *The Art of Collecting Vintage Omega*
A collector's guide to navigating the vintage Omega market with confidence and knowledge.

The Hunt

112 | *Six Objects of Desire for the Discerning Collector*
Your biannual guide to the acquisitions that matter. We don't feature what's readily available—only the objects worth pursuing with determination, patience, and proper expertise.

Final Thought

118 | On the Art of Keeping Time
Reflections on what makes a timepiece worthy of a collection.

THE CONNOISSEUR

#1 December 2025 - June 2026

Editor-In-Chief
Robert Buratti

Art Direction
Sub Rosa Studio

Subscriptions
info@theconnoisseur.au

Advertising
advertising@theconnoisseur.au

Produced & Published by
Buratti Art Group

Director & Founder
Robert Buratti

Contributors
Robert Buratti, James Master, Jo Wiggins. Jonathan Maine, Jenna Coleman, Ella Tomlin

Reproduction in whole or in part is not permitted without the written authorisation of the publisher. In the reproduction of artworks and products all reasonable efforts have been made to trace copyright holders where appropriate.

ISBN 978-0-6452089-5-5

The Connoisseur acknowledges and pays respect to the Noogar people of the Boorloo Nation, custodians of the land on which we operate.

IMAGES: Grand vin de Lafite. Courtesy Rothschild | Tim Storrier in the studio. Courtesy the artist & Gary Grealy | Omega Speedmaster. Courtesy Buratti Art

THE BRIEF

Death of the Impulse Purchase

Why the most sophisticated collectors are spending more time researching and less time buying.

JONATHON MAINE

The phone call came at 2 AM. A veteran watch dealer in Geneva had secured something extraordinary—a pristine 1967 Rolex Daytona with the right papers, the right patina, everything a serious collector dreams about. The price was fair, but the window was narrow. Did his client want it?

Ten years ago, the answer would have been immediate. Today, it took three weeks. Welcome to the era of the considered acquisition, where the world's most sophisticated collectors have transformed patience from virtue into strategy. The impulsive purchase—once the hallmark of passion and means—is dying. In its place: a methodical, research-intensive approach that's reshaping every corner of the luxury market.

The New Collecting Calculus

The shift isn't about diminished desire or shallower pockets. It's about information overload meeting market maturity. Today's serious collector has access to auction databases going back decades, online forums dissecting every detail, and Instagram accounts documenting comparable pieces in real-time. The mystique that once surrounded rare objects has been replaced by radical transparency.

"Twenty years ago, you relied on your dealer's word and your gut," says Margaret Chen, who advises high-net-worth clients on art acquisitions. "Now my clients arrive with spreadsheets. They know what a piece sold for in 1997, who owned it in between, and what condition issues to look for. The romance hasn't disappeared—it's just been delayed."

This delay is everything. Where wealthy buyers once competed on speed—who

---

The informed buyer is a less emotional buyer, and emotion drives prices. The premium paid for certainty—for having done all the research—is often lower than the premium once paid for desire alone.

---

could say yes fastest—they now compete on diligence. The question has shifted from "Can I afford it?" to "Should I own it?" And answering that question properly takes time.

What Research Means Now

Modern collecting research extends far beyond authentication and provenance. Collectors are investigating:

Market trajectory: Not just what something costs today, but where its category is headed. Is Japanese whisky peaking? Are 1990s sports cars undervalued? Will young collectors care about this artist in twenty years?

Opportunity cost: Every acquisition means passing on others. Sophisticated collectors increasingly think in terms of portfolio balance across categories—wine, watches, art, design—rather than isolated purchases.

Exit strategy: Even collectors who insist they're buying to keep forever are researching liquidity. The ability to sell matters, even if you never intend to.

The maker's trajectory: For contemporary work, collectors are studying artists' and craftspeople's careers with the intensity once reserved for tech stocks. Who are they showing with? What institutions are acquiring their work? How deep is their practice? This level of scrutiny would have been impossible a generation ago. Now it's table stakes.

The Dealer's Dilemma

For dealers, this shift is transformative—and not entirely welcome. The traditional model relied on relationships, expertise, and yes, a certain information asymmetry. Dealers knew more than clients, and that knowledge commanded both respect and margin. Today's informed collector has eroded that advantage. But paradoxically, the best dealers are busier than ever.

"The clients who succeed in this environment aren't trying to replace dealers—they're trying to become better partners with them," explains Thomas Marks, a London-based specialist in 20th century design. "They do their homework, then they come to me for the insights that databases can't provide. The human element matters more, not less."

What's changed is the nature of that human element. Dealers are evolving from gatekeepers to consultants, from sources of information to interpreters of it. The value proposition has shifted from "I can get you this" to "I can tell you whether you should want this."

The Auction Adjustment

Auction houses are feeling the shift acutely. The theater of the sale room—the raised paddle, the winning bid, the rush—loses some luster when every lot has been analyzed to exhaustion before the gavel falls.

Major houses have responded by frontloading more information than ever: condition reports that read like dissertations, live video examinations, and detailed provenance research that would have been considered excessive a decade ago. They're not fighting the trend toward deliberation; they're enabling it.

But something has been lost. The informed buyer is a less emotional buyer, and emotion drives prices. The premium paid for certainty—for having done all the research—is often lower than the premium once paid for desire alone.

For living artists, designers, and craftspeople, the implications are profound. The contemporary market increasingly rewards those who document their work obsessively: process, materials, inspiration, everything. A piece without a story is a piece that stalls in the research phase.

"I spend as much time on provenance creation as I do on the work itself," admits Sarah Wu, a ceramicist whose pieces command five figures. "High-resolution photos of every stage, detailed material sourcing, documentation of influences. My collectors aren't just buying an object—they're buying a complete intellectual property package."

This isn't mere marketing. It's recognizing that contemporary collecting has become a form of investment in cultural production, and investors want documentation.

The Psychological Shift

Perhaps most significantly, the death of the impulse purchase reflects a broader cultural reckoning with acquisition itself. Wealthy collectors increasingly see their collections as legacy projects rather than accumulation exercises. Each piece must justify its place not just aesthetically or financially, but philosophically.

"I ask myself: would I want my grandchildren to inherit this understanding why I bought it?" says one collector who requested anonymity.

"If I can't articulate that clearly, I'm not ready to acquire."

This mindset transforms collecting from consumption into curation, from having into being. It's slower, more deliberate, arguably more meaningful.

What Comes Next

The considered acquisition isn't without costs. Markets that rely on velocity—auction houses, dealers with high inventory turnover, artists who need volume—are adjusting painfully. The most exclusive makers now have waitlists measured in years, not because they can't produce faster, but because clients aren't ready to buy faster.

Meanwhile, the gap widens between informed and uninformed buyers. Those who haven't adapted to research-intensive collecting increasingly find themselves outmaneuvered, paying premiums for pieces that sophisticated collectors passed on after proper diligence.

The future belongs to the patient. The impulsive collector, armed with capital but not knowledge, is becoming a relic—sometimes profitable for sellers, but increasingly rare.

That 2 AM phone call about the Daytona? The client eventually bought it. But only after commissioning an independent condition report, consulting three other collectors, reviewing five years of comparable sales data, and honestly assessing whether his collection needed another Rolex. He's glad he did the work. The watch is perfect. But more importantly, he knows exactly why he owns it.

And that knowledge, in the end, matters more than the watch itself.

"The clients who succeed in this environment aren't trying to replace dealers—they're trying to become better partners with them," ... "They do their homework, then they come to me for the insights that databases can't provide. The human element matters more, not less." ~ *Thomas Marks*

The Brief welcomes responses and counter-arguments. Have you made an impulse purchase you regret—or treasure? Write to us at editor@theconnoisseur.com.au

THE BRIEF

Wine Investing for Beginners: Don't

A contrarian take: why buying wine to drink (not flip) makes you a better collector and a happier person

JONATHON MAINE

Here's what the wine investment advocates won't tell you: the spreadsheet ruins the wine.

I learned this the hard way. Ten years ago, flush with a bonus and impressed by articles about fine wine outperforming the S&P 500, I bought a case of 2009 Bordeaux futures. Top château, impeccable provenance, perfect storage. On paper, it was flawless.

I never opened a single bottle. Every time I considered it, I'd check the current market price. The wine had appreciated nicely—15% annually. Opening a bottle meant "losing" $400 in potential profit. So the case sat, accumulating value I couldn't taste and satisfaction I never felt. Eventually I sold it. Made a decent return, paid some capital gains tax, and felt absolutely nothing. The wine had become a ticker symbol with a cork.

That's when I understood: wine investing and wine collecting are not just different activities. They're opposing philosophies that cannot coexist in the same cellar.

The Seduction of Returns

The pitch is intoxicating. Blue-chip Burgundy has returned 147% over the past decade. First-growth Bordeaux tracks with alternative assets. Rare whisky outpaced gold. The data is real, the returns documented, the opportunity seemingly obvious. For professional investors with climate-controlled warehouses, insurance policies, and no emotional attachment to liquid assets, fine wine can indeed be a legitimate alternative investment. But they're not reading this article. You are, and if you're a beginner seduced by wine investment stories, you're about to make several expensive mistakes that have nothing to do with choosing the wrong vintage.

What They Don't Tell You

First, the costs. Professional storage isn't optional—wine is a fragile asset that turns to expensive vinegar in poor conditions. Factor in insurance, authentication, eventual auction fees, and shipping. Real returns are significantly lower than headline figures suggest.

Second, liquidity. Try selling three bottles of anything. The market wants full cases, preferably in original wooden cases, with perfect provenance. That half-case you opened two bottles from? Worth significantly less than six-twelfths of a full case. Wine investment requires volume most beginners can't afford.

Third, expertise. The Liv-ex Fine Wine 100 index tracks specific wines from specific vintages. Buying the right château from the wrong year, or the right year from the wrong château, means market-lagging returns. Professionals spend careers developing this knowledge. You're competing against them with a subscription to *Wine Spectator*. But the real cost is subtler and more devastating: wine investment kills the joy that made you interested in wine in the first place.

The Collector vs. The Investor

A collector buys wine to drink it—eventually, thoughtfully, at the right moment with the right people. The collection is a library of future experiences, each bottle a promise of pleasure deferred. An investor buys wine to sell it. Each bottle is a commodity whose value exists entirely on paper. The wine itself becomes irrelevant—it could be Château Margaux or crude oil. What matters is the spread between purchase and sale price.

These mindsets cannot coexist. Once you start tracking your cellar's market value, every bottle opened is a loss realised. Sharing a great wine with friends becomes an act of financial self-harm. The anniversary dinner where you finally open that special bottle? You've just consumed your quarterly returns. This is madness. Wine exists to be drunk. The moment you forget that, you've stopped being a collector and become something sadder: a speculator hoarding pleasure you're too anxious to consume. I rebuilt my cellar with a different philosophy: buy what you want to drink, from producers you want to support, at prices that won't haunt you when the cork comes out. This approach has several advantages the investment guides never mention.

You learn faster. Opening bottles—even expensive ones—teaches you about regions, vintages, winemaking styles, and your own preferences. That education is impossible if everything stays sealed pending market conditions.

You build relationships. Call a winemaker and say "I loved your 2018, I'd like to buy more" and you're a customer. Say "I'm buying your futures as an investment" and you're a commodity trader. Guess which one gets allocated the limited releases? You actually enjoy it. The point of wine is pleasure—the taste, certainly, but also the ritual, the conversation, the memories

THE BRIEF

THE BRIEF

created around great bottles. None of that appears on a balance sheet, and all of it matters more than appreciation rates - and paradoxically, you often end up with more valuable wine. Not because you're chasing investment-grade bottles, but because you're buying what you genuinely love, often from small producers before the market catches up. Passion tends to outperform spreadsheets over time.

The One Exception

There is exactly one good reason for a beginner to buy wine as an investment: to fund future drinking. Buy young wine you can't yet afford to drink. Store it properly. As it matures and appreciates, sell half to finance opening the rest. This approach—sometimes called "drinking on the house"—uses investment logic to subsidise collecting. It requires patience, knowledge, and capital. But it keeps the wine's ultimate purpose in focus. You're not hoarding financial instruments; you're time-shifting pleasure and letting the market help fund it.

If you're drawn to wine collecting, here's my advice: forget everything you've read about investment returns. Start by drinking widely and taking notes. Spend $20-$50 per bottle and explore. Learn what you actually like, not what the critics say you should like. Once you've developed opinions, start buying slightly more than you'll drink immediately. Build a modest cellar of wines you're excited to open—some for weeknights, some for special occasions, all purchased because you want to drink them. If bottles appreciate while aging in your cellar, wonderful. But that's a side effect, not the goal. The goal is to have great wine available when you want it, purchased at prices that made sense when you bought it. Track your purchases if you must, but track them by drinking window, not market value. Organise by region, style, or occasion—anything except current auction prices. And for the love of terroir,

open the good bottles. Life is too short and wine is too precious to let either sit idle while you monitor index funds.

The Bottom Line

The truly wealthy don't invest in wine—they simply buy what they want to drink and never think about the cost. The rest of us need to make choices. But those choices should be about pleasure, knowledge, and experience, not capital appreciation. Every bottle you

---

Start by drinking widely and taking notes. Spend $20-$50 per bottle and explore. Learn what you actually like, not what the critics say you should like.

---

open is an opportunity to learn something, share something, or celebrate something. Every bottle you hoard for investment returns is an opportunity missed. Ten years after my Bordeaux experiment, my cellar is worth less on paper and vastly more in every way that matters.

I know more, I've shared more, and I've drunk things I'll remember forever. The investment returns I gave up are a rounding error compared to what I gained. So by all means, buy good wine. Buy more than you need. Let it age. Build a collection.

Just remember: if you're checking market prices before deciding whether to open a bottle, you're no longer a collector. You're a fund manager who's forgotten what the portfolio is for, and that's the saddest kind of

In Defense of the Copy

When is an homage acceptable, and when does it cross into theft? A nuanced look at inspiration, appropriation, and the murky ethics of design borrowing.

JO WIGGINS

The watch on my wrist costs $400. It has a bidirectional rotating bezel, a date window at three o'clock, and a silhouette that unmistakably evokes the Rolex Submariner—a watch that costs thirty times more and currently has a two-year waiting list.

Am I wearing a tribute? An homage? A knockoff? Or am I complicit in intellectual property theft?

The answer, it turns out, depends entirely on whom you ask. And that ambiguity reveals something fascinating about how we value originality, innovation, and the right to be inspired by what came before.

Every serious collector has a line. On one side: legitimate inspiration and design evolution. On the other: crass copying that deserves contempt. The problem is that no two collectors draw that line in the same place.

Consider the automotive world. The Porsche 911's silhouette has been essentially unchanged since 1963—yet dozens of manufacturers have created sports cars with rear engines, sloping rooflines, and circular headlights. Some we celebrate as part of the German sports car tradition. Others we dismiss as derivative.

Perhaps the real question isn't about copies at all. It's about how we value originality in an age of infinite reproducibility.

Or furniture: Eames-style loungers flood the market at every price point. The original commands $8,000 and up; copies start at $800. The design is iconic, the patents long expired. Is buying the copy an act of democratic access to good design, or an insult to the original creators' legacy?

The watch world offers perhaps the murkiest waters. Swiss manufacturers openly borrow design cues from each other—Omega's Seamaster and Rolex's Submariner have been in conversation for seventy years. Yet when a Chinese manufacturer creates a near-identical replica, the industry cries foul. Where exactly is the ethical boundary?

The Case for Copies

Let's start with an unpopular position: not all copying is bad, and some of it is necessary for culture to progress.

Design evolution requires iteration. The first dive watch influenced the second, which influenced the third. The first modernist chair informed a generation of furniture designers. If we'd locked down every design innovation with impenetrable intellectual property protections, we'd have less innovation, not more.

"People forget that many 'original' designs were themselves synthesizing earlier ideas," notes David Hammond, a design historian. "The Eames lounge chair drew from traditional club chairs. The Submariner evolved from military dive watches. Even the most iconic designs have antecedents."

There's also a democratic argument. The original Wassily chair costs thousands; a well-made reproduction costs hundreds. Should great design be accessible only to the wealthy? Or is there virtue in bringing strong design to a broader market?

The watch world is particularly relevant here. A mechanical Rolex Submariner performs essentially the same function as a $400 automatic homage watch. Both tell time, both are water resistant, both use similar movements. The $9,000 premium buys heritage, exclusivity, and finishing—intangibles that matter to collectors but not to function. If someone wants the aesthetic and functionality without the brand cache or investment, why should we judge that choice harshly?

Where the Line Gets Crossed

Yet even as I make that argument, I feel its weakness. Because there is a line, and when you see it crossed, you know.

The line is deception. An homage declares itself openly—different branding, honest pricing, transparent about its inspiration. A counterfeit deceives, bearing fake logos

THE BRIEF

and falsified paperwork, sold as the genuine article to unsuspecting buyers.

But there's a subtler line too: the one between inspiration and parasitism.

Consider the difference between two approaches to copying the Eames lounge chair. Company A studies the original, learns its proportions, and creates a chair that evokes the same comfort and aesthetic while using different materials and construction methods. Company B simply replicates the exact specifications, sources similar materials, and produces as close to an identical copy as possible without triggering lawsuits. Both are legal once patents expire. But Company A is engaging with design; Company B is merely reproducing it.

"The question isn't whether you borrowed—everyone borrows," explains Sarah Chen, an intellectual property attorney specializing in design. "It's whether you added anything. Did you synthesise inspiration into something new, or did you just photocopy?"

The Maker's Perspective

Talk to actual designers and craftspeople, and the ethics become even more complicated. Many established makers acknowledge their debts openly. They'll point to the pieces that inspired them, the craftspeople they apprenticed under, the design movements they're extending. Influence, in this context, is honorable—provided it's acknowledged.

"I'm deeply influenced by mid-century Scandinavian furniture," says Martin Weber, a contemporary furniture maker. "But I'm not trying to replicate it. I'm trying to have a conversation with it. That distinction matters to me." The designers who feel most violated by copying are often those whose work is most recent. When a living designer creates something, then sees it reproduced cheaply within months, the sting isn't just economic—

it's personal. The copy doesn't just compete with the original; it devalues the creative process itself.

Yet here's the paradox: those same designers will adamantly defend their right to be influenced by historical work. Inspiration from the past is research; inspiration from the present is theft. The difference is less about ethics than timing.

The Collector's Dilemma

So what's a conscientious collector to do? Some adopt absolutist positions: only originals, never copies, regardless of price or availability. This has the virtue of clarity but requires either deep pockets or narrow interests. It also implicitly argues that design should remain exclusive, which sits uncomfortably with egalitarian values.

Others take a pragmatic approach: originals when possible, quality reproductions when not. A vintage Eames if you can find one in good condition; a licensed reproduction if you can't. A Rolex if the waiting list and price align with your budget; a well-made homage if they don't. The most nuanced position—and the hardest to maintain—is contextual judgment. Ask: Is this maker adding value or just extracting it? Are they engaging with design history or exploiting it? Would the original designer see this as flattery or theft?

These aren't easy questions, and honest people will answer differently.

What We Owe Originality

Perhaps the real question isn't about copies at all. It's about how we value originality in an age of infinite reproducibility.

The original Submariner isn't better at telling time than its homages. The original Eames chair isn't more comfortable than quality reproductions. What you're paying for is originality itself—the idea, the innovation, the first instance of solving a problem in a particular way.

And maybe that's worth paying for, even when cheaper alternatives exist. Not because the function is superior, but because supporting original work ensures there will be more of it. Every time we choose the copy over the original purely on price, we're making a small vote against innovation.

But we're also making a small vote for accessibility. And both values matter.

I still wear that $400 watch sometimes. I also own a Rolex, purchased after years of saving and waiting. Both have a place in my collection, and I've made peace with that contradiction. The copy taught me what I valued in the design. It let me live with the aesthetic before committing significant resources. When I finally acquired the original, I understood why it commanded its premium—not just intellectually, but viscerally. Would I have reached the same appreciation without the copy? Probably not. Does that justify the copy's existence? I'm honestly not sure. What I am sure of is this: anyone who tells you the ethics of copying are simple is either not thinking carefully or trying to sell you something—whether that's an expensive original or a cheap reproduction.

The truth, as usual, lives in the uncomfortable space between clear answers. And that's exactly where thoughtful collectors should be willing to dwell.

Where do you draw the line? Share your perspective at editor@theconnoisseur.au

THE BRIEF

The Quiet Revolution in Hotel Luxury

Why the world's most discerning travellers are abandoning mega-resorts for intimate properties with 10 rooms or less.

JO WIGGINS

At Passalacqua on Lake Como, there are just 24 rooms. Each is individually designed in an 18th-century villa that once housed Pope Innocent XI. There's no assembly-line check-in experience. The staff knows your name—and remembers it. In 2024, it was named the Best Hotel in Europe by The World's 50 Best Hotels.

This is luxury hospitality's quiet revolution. Across Europe, Japan, Australia, and the Americas, sophisticated travellers—the ones who could afford any property, book any experience—are increasingly choosing intimate hotels with fewer than 30 rooms over branded establishments with hundreds. It's not about rejecting luxury. It's about redefining it.

What Changed

The mega-resort promised everything: multiple restaurants, elaborate spas, curated activities, staff to fulfil any whim. For decades, "luxury" meant more—more amenities, more choices, more square footage, more everything.

But in recent years, a critical mass of well-travelled guests have decided that more wasn't actually better. It was just more.

In Japan, luxury ryokans like Beniya Mukayu offer just 16 rooms in a serene environment, earning recognition as the Best Small Hotel Spa Worldwide in 2015. In Rome, Villa Spalletti Trivelli provides only 14 rooms, yet delivers an experience that larger hotels cannot match. The Donatella Boutique Hotel in Miami Beach operates with merely six rooms yet employs 60 staff members—a ratio that would be economically impossible at scale.

That level of personalised attention is mathematically impossible at a 200-room property. Small hotels—fewer than 30 rooms—operate on entirely different logic. They're not hospitality businesses trying to scale down; they're intimate spaces that happen to accommodate guests. The distinction matters enormously.

The Economics of Intimacy

Counterintuitively, these small properties often charge more per night than their large luxury competitors. Historic ryokans like Asaba in Japan's Izu Peninsula command premium rates for their beautiful rooms, soothing onsen, and personalised service. The premium isn't for thread count or square footage. It's for something harder to quantify: the feeling of being a houseguest rather than a customer.

Small properties can do things impossible for chains. The chef sources ingredients based on your specific dietary preferences. Proprietors design itineraries based on their actual relationships with local artisans, not commission arrangements with tour operators. Breakfast happens when you want it, not between 7 and 10 AM.

This level of customisation requires low volume and high margins. You're not paying for luxury; you're paying for undivided attention.

The Owners, Not Operators

Bill Kimpton pioneered the American boutique hotel concept in the 1980s after travelling through Europe and staying at small hotels where you get to know the owners, have wine in the lobby, and everything was personable and intimate. His frustration with impersonal American hotels led him to open The Bedford Hotel in San Francisco in 1981—America's first boutique hotel.

Today's most compelling small hotels continue this tradition. French designer Christian Louboutin opened a 13-room luxury boutique hotel in Melides, Portugal, whilst Ralph Lauren introduced his signature style with a 36-room boutique property at Round Hill Hotel & Villas in Jamaica. These aren't amateur operations—the execution is often more polished than branded hotels. But the motivation is different. These owners aren't optimising for revenue per available room or occupancy rates. They're creating experiences they themselves would want.

At Sowaka in Kyoto, the 108 Garden View Suite in a renovated century-old building showcases designers' exquisite attention to detail in every aspect. This isn't about following brand standards. It's about personal vision.

What's Lost, What's Gained

Small hotels sacrifice things many travellers consider essential. There's no room service at 2 AM. No concierge desk with multilingual staff. No bellhop to handle your seven pieces of luggage.

If you arrive expecting the full-service infrastructure of a Four Seasons, you'll be disappointed.

But what you gain is irreplaceable. At properties like Gora Kadan in Hakone, built on the former summer villa of the Imperial Family, guests experience views of the mountainside from every room and access to private onsen baths. Real conversations with people who live interesting lives.

Introduction to their neighbours, their suppliers, their favourite hidden spots. The experience of a place as an insider rather than a tourist.

The best small properties don't just offer a room—they offer admission to a life you couldn't access otherwise. That's worth more than any amenity list.

The Future of Five-Star

The major hotel groups are watching this trend nervously. Hyatt acquired the London-based Mr & Mrs Smith for £53 million in 2023, aiming to expand its luxury and boutique hotel offerings, adding properties in 20 countries where the hotel giant was previously not present. Minor Hotels expanded its footprint in the boutique luxury market in December 2023 with acquisitions across the Asia-Pacific region.

Some chains are launching "boutique" sub-brands, trying to bottle intimacy at scale. It rarely works authentically. You can't train staff to provide the authenticity that comes from an owner-operator who genuinely cares.

The boutique hotel market was valued at $9.8 billion in 2023 and is expected to reach $18 billion by 2033, driven by increasing consumer demand for customised and distinctive travel experiences, particularly from Millennials and Gen Z travellers.

This is hospitality returning to its original meaning: the act of welcoming strangers with generosity. And in an age of industrialised travel, that personal touch has become the ultimate luxury.

Discovered a small hotel that changed how you travel? Tell us at editor@theconnoisseur.au

New Discoveries

Exploring the exceptional, the unexpected, and the extraordinary from Australia and beyond. This month, we uncover a grape-based gin from Margaret River, a First Nations fashion game-changer and a re-released classic.

NEW DISCOVERIES

NEW DISCOVERIES

When Yolŋu Art Becomes High Fashion

Bula'bula Arts Centre x Black Cat Couture

WORDS | JENNA COLEMAN

A groundbreaking fashion collaboration between Bula'bula Arts and Black Cat Couture brings Yolnu art to the runway.

When over 20 Ramingining artists gathered to paint panels of fabric, they weren't just creating art—they were embarking on a journey that would transform their traditional work into wearable masterpieces. The result is 'Garkambarryirri' (Daybreak), a stunning collection that graced the Country to Couture runway at the 2025 National Indigenous Fashion Awards, representing a deepening creative partnership between Bula'bula Arts Centre and Black Cat Couture designer Marcia Russell.

This collaboration stands apart in the Australian fashion landscape, not simply for its beauty, but for the profound cultural exchange and trust it represents. Building on their successful 2024 debut collection 'Soar', the partnership has evolved into something more adventurous, more confident, and more willing to push boundaries while remaining firmly rooted in Yolŋu culture.

The genesis of this collaboration traces back to 2023, when Russell was teaching sewing skills at Ramingining School through the Families as First Teachers program. Her regular visits to Bula'bula Arts Centre sparked an idea: what if the exquisite work of these traditional artists could be incorporated into high fashion? The concept wasn't without its challenges. Many of the artists had never painted directly onto fabric or seen their work transformed into three-dimensional garments. There was uncertainty about whether they would engage with the project. But when the first piece emerged—"like a phoenix from the pile of fabric and vintage sewing patterns," as Russell describes it—everything changed. The artists were enthralled.

What is it? A high-fashion collection featuring hand-painted panels by over 20 Yolŋu artists from Ramingining, incorporated into bespoke garments by Black Cat Couture designer Marcia Russell.

Where do I find it? The collection was presented at Country to Couture 2025. Individual pieces are completely bespoke and one-of-a-kind. For inquiries about future collaborations or commissions, contact Bula'bula Arts Centre in Ramingining, Northern Territory, or Black Cat Couture.

How much should I pay? These are unique, wearable art pieces featuring multiple days of hand-painting by renowned Yolŋu artists on premium silk and linen. Expect pricing to reflect the significant artistic labor, high-quality materials, and bespoke nature of each garment—these are investment pieces and collector's items.

How should it be enjoyed? These garments are designed to be worn and celebrated. Each piece tells a story rooted in Yolŋu culture and the 'Garkambarryirri' (Daybreak) theme. While suitable for special occasions and high-fashion events, they're meant to be experienced as living art—a three-dimensional expression of traditional culture meeting contemporary design. Consider them wearable masterpieces that honor both the artists' heritage and the collaborative creative process.

NEW DISCOVERIES

NEW DISCOVERIES

The High-Beat Pioneer Returns
Longines Ultra-Chron Classic

WORDS | ROBERT BURATTI

A meticulously faithful revival of a 1967 high-beat icon that reminds us why Longines matters

When watch enthusiasts discuss high-beat mechanical movements, the conversation typically turns to Zenith's El Primero or Grand Seiko's legendary calibres. Yet this overlooks a crucial piece of horological history: Longines was there first. Long before these celebrated movements, Longines had been quietly pioneering high-frequency watchmaking, and the new Ultra-Chron Classic serves as a potent reminder of this often-forgotten legacy.

The story begins far earlier than most realise. In 1910, Longines patented a stopwatch capable of measuring 1/10th of a second—a 5Hz frequency that was revolutionary for its time. By 1916, they had pushed this to an astonishing 50Hz. In 1959, they developed the first high-beat movement for a wristwatch, an observatory chronometer that set new accuracy records. And in 1967—two years before Zenith's famed El Primero—Longines launched the Ultra-Chron collection with reference 7827, the first high-beat watch produced in large volumes, guaranteed to an accuracy of two seconds per day. Outstanding then, impressive even by today's standards.

The 2025 Ultra-Chron Classic is an uncannily faithful recreation of that original 7827, looking so authentically 1960s that it could have been plucked straight from your grandfather's watch box. Every detail evokes the era: the thick, domed crystal; the sector dial with polished indices; the applied logos and dial text; the all-silver color scheme. It's vintage aesthetics executed with modern precision. But look closer, and state-of-the-art updates reveal themselves. That crystal is sapphire, not acrylic. The folding clasp features micro-adjustment. You get the romance of a 1960s design without the fragility of an actual vintage watch—all the quality-of-life improvements that make it competitive as a modern daily wearer.

Longines offers the Ultra-Chron Classic in two sizes: a period-appropriate 37mm (the original was technically 35mm, or 37mm with crown) and a more contemporary 40mm. Both measure a svelte 10.5mm thick and come on either a black alligator leather strap with pin buckle or a fittingly retro five-link bracelet that could have come straight from the 1960s.

What is it? A faithful recreation of Longines› pioneering 1967 Ultra-Chron reference 7827, the first high-beat watch produced in large volumes.

Where do I find it? Available now from authorised Longines dealers worldwide.

How much should I pay? A$5,825 on black alligator leather strap; A$6,000 on stainless steel bracelet. This positions it competitively within the premium Swiss watch segment while offering chronometer certification that exceeds COSC standards.

How should it be enjoyed? As a versatile dressy daily wearer that transitions seamlessly from office to evening. The silver sunray dial and retro aesthetic pair beautifully with both formal and smart-casual attire. The 50-meter water resistance means you need not baby it, while the high-beat movement and TIMELAB certification ensure it's accurate enough for those who appreciate precision.

NEW DISCOVERIES

Where River Grapes meet Coastal Botanicals
Wise Gin

WORDS | **JAMES MASTER**

Margaret River's coastal spirit captures the essence of Western Australia in every small-batch bottle

In the sun-drenched wine country of Margaret River, Western Australia, a distinctive spirit is making waves beyond the region's celebrated wine scene. Wise Gin, crafted by the established Wise Wine estate, represents a bold venture into artisan distilling that leverages the area's unique terroir and botanical riches.

What sets Wise Gin apart from the crowded craft gin market is its uncommon base: premium Margaret River grapes. Rather than following the traditional grain-based approach, the distillers at Wise have created a spirit that bridges their winemaking heritage with contemporary gin craft. This grape foundation lends a subtle smoothness and complexity that distinguishes these gins from their conventional counterparts.

The production takes place on-site at the Wise Winery and Distillery in Eagle Bay, where custom-built stills produce small batches through a triple-distillation process. This meticulous approach ensures consistency and purity, while the intimate scale allows for experimentation and attention to detail that larger operations simply cannot match.

The brand's commitment to showcasing native Australian botanicals gives each expression a genuine sense of place. The coastal character that defines these gins isn't merely marketing—it's the product of ingredients sourced from the surrounding landscape, capturing the rugged beauty of where the Indian Ocean meets ancient forests.

The **Signature Gin** serves as an ideal introduction to the range, with bright citrus notes from lemon myrtle and orange peel creating a refreshing, approachable spirit that works beautifully in classic cocktails or simply with quality tonic water.

For those seeking something more adventurous, the **Mandarin Gin** offers an intriguing sweet profile with lingering mandarin flavors that some have compared to Cointreau, making it particularly versatile for both sipping and mixing. Meanwhile, the **Pink Gin** takes a sophisticated approach to the popular category, using real strawberries to achieve a clean, dry style with just a whisper of sweetness at the finish—worlds away from the cloying sweetness of some competitors.

What is it? A premium small-batch Australian gin crafted from Margaret River grapes and native botanicals, triple-distilled in custom stills at Wise Winery and Distillery.

Where do I find it? Visit the Wise Winery and Distillery tasting room in Eagle Bay, Margaret River, Western Australia, where you can sample and purchase the full range.

How much should I pay? Pricing varies by expression and retailer, but expect to pay premium craft gin prices reflective of the small-batch production and quality ingredients.

How should it be enjoyed? The Signature Gin shines in a classic gin and tonic with quality tonic water and a citrus garnish. The Mandarin Gin works beautifully in citrus-forward cocktails or over ice. Pink Gin is delightful served simply with tonic and fresh strawberries.

NEW DISCOVERIES

LUXURY INTELLIGENCE | *Market*

Luxury Market Intelligence

DECEMBER 2025

Art Basel Miami kicks off December 3. Japanese whisky is up 80%. Hermès Birkins trade at triple retail. The 1990s Porsche market has gone mad. Wine prices are finally bottoming. And if you're still trying to flip watches for profit, you've already lost. Here's what sophisticated collectors are actually buying right now—and why the smartest money is moving while everyone else watches.

LUXURY INTELLIGENCE | *Market*

AUCTION

LUXURY INTELLIGENCE

December 2025 presents a watershed moment for luxury collecting. **Art Basel Miami runs December 3-7** with 287 galleries from 44 countries, while major auction houses stage significant December sales across art, watches, and wine. The luxury market has stabilised after pandemic volatility, with **Japanese whisky up 80%**, **Hermès Birkins trading at 2-3x retail**, and **air-cooled Porsches appreciating at astronomical rates**. Market corrections in wine and art create compelling buying opportunities, while watch collecting shifts toward independent makers and precious metals. The overarching trend: genuine collectors replacing speculators, premiumization across categories, and younger buyers (under 40) driving 60% of transactions.

December 2025 auction calendar and fair season

The December luxury calendar centers on Miami Art Week and strategic auction placements. **Art Basel Miami Beach opens December 3** with VIP previews, followed by public days December 5-7 at the Miami Beach Convention Center. This year's fair showcases 287 premier galleries including Gagosian, Hauser & Wirth, and David Zwirner, with notable first-time representations from Cuba (El Apartamento) and Ukraine (Voloshyn Gallery). The inaugural Art Basel Awards will honor Gold Medalists during the fair. **Design Miami** runs concurrently December 2-7, celebrating its 20th anniversary under the curatorial theme «Make. Believe.» with director Glenn Adamson emphasizing acts of innovation.

Phillips leads December auction activity with **The New York Watch Auction: XIII on December 6-7** in New York, building on their record-breaking 2024 performance that achieved four consecutive «white glove» (100% sold) sales totaling

ABOVE: Stephen Friedman Gallery Art Basel Miami Beach

$53.7 million. Sotheby's stages **Important Watches December 8** in New York during Luxury Week, while conducting **Abu Dhabi Collectors' Week December 2-5** coinciding with the Grand Prix. The Abu Dhabi event features the Precision & Brilliance sale December 5, headlined by **The Desert Rose—a 31.86-carat fancy vivid orangy pink diamond** estimated at $5-7 million, the largest ever graded in this category.

Wine auctions include **Acker's Hong Kong sale December 6** featuring the finest and rarest wines, and **Hart Davis Hart's two-day auction December 18-19**. Hart Davis Hart remains the #1 U.S. wine auction house with over $900 million sold across 160+ auctions. Phillips also conducts Modern & Contemporary Art auctions online December 2-16, along with New Now contemporary art December 2 in London and New York Jewels online December 1-10.

Miami Art Week extends far beyond the main fairs, with satellite events including UNTITLED Art, Art Miami, NADA Miami, SCOPE Miami Beach, and dozens more spanning December 1-7 across Miami Beach, Wynwood, and the Design District. Collector sentiment remains strong despite 2024's 12% market decline, with **83.9% sell-through rates** at major auctions indicating genuine demand.

Japanese Whisky, Hermès, and Porsche lead alternative investments

The Japanese whisky market reached **$995 million in 2025**, projected to hit

LUXURY INTELLIGENCE

The 1990s Porsche market—specifically the 993 generation representing the last air-cooled 911—shows remarkable strength. **Standard 993 Carreras average £61,266** ($77,824), with an 85% sell-through rate. The **Turbo S commands £404,700** (~$515,000), while the ultimate **993 GT2 trades between $665,000 and $2.4 million**, with pristine examples at $800,000-$1 million. Only 57 street-version GT2s were produced from the 194 total run. The "last air-cooled" designation creates cachet that drives astronomical appreciation rates. Days of $20,000 911SCs have vanished; standard 964s now exceed $60,000. Collectors prioritise low-mileage, well-documented examples in desirable colours (Speed Yellow, Arena Red, Midnight Blue), with manual transmissions commanding premiums over Tiptronic.

Beyond these three categories, **vintage Rolex appreciates 550%** on average from 2010 to 2025, with the Submariner 116610 up 335% and GMT-Master 1675 up 325%. Luxury sneaker resale reached **$6 billion in the U.S.**, potentially $30 billion globally by 2030, though the market matured with only 47% of releases trading above retail. Chanel's Classic Medium Flap increased to **$11,300** (up 4% from 2024), demonstrating prestige pricing to maintain exclusivity. Contemporary art shows selective strength, with emerging artists like Yu Nishimura, Louis Fratino, and Emma McIntyre achieving record auction prices while the broader market contracted 12%.

Luxury Openings

The past six months brought transformative luxury openings globally. **The Chancery Rosewood opened September 1** in London's Mayfair, converting the former U.S. Embassy into 144 all-suite accommodations—Rosewood's first all-suite property.

$1.8 billion by 2033, with aged whisky demand surging 80% and limited-edition sales up 300%. Yamazaki dominates valuations: the **55-Year-Old commands $953,237** (only 200 bottles produced), while the 25-Year-Old retail price jumped from ¥160,000 to ¥360,000, with secondary market prices exceeding $20,000. The **Yamazaki 18-Year-Old earned Supreme Champion Spirit 2025**, with prices up 211% since 2016. Suntory invested $10 billion in distillery upgrades, yet supply constraints won't ease until 2031. Investment outlook remains bullish: the Rare Whisky 101 Japanese 100 Index appreciated 580% since 2014, though recent retail price increases of 50-125% risk pricing out aspirational buyers.

Hermès bags continue their unprecedented appreciation trajectory. The **Birkin 25 Togo now costs $12,700** at U.S. retail (up 6% from 2024, 29% since 2016), but secondary markets command $28,000-$30,000—a 2.4x premium. The **Mini Kelly achieves 3x retail** at $28,000-$33,000, while the Kelly Pochette reaches 4.5x at approximately $30,000, the highest premium in luxury handbags. Matte alligator versions sell for $54,000-$66,000 at auction versus €30,000 retail. Market dynamics shifted dramatically: Hermès eliminated formal waitlists, requiring annual purchase history that «restarts every year,» forcing longtime clients to demonstrate continued loyalty. May 2025 brought additional 4.4-5.9% U.S. price increases due to tariffs. Despite luxury market softness, Hermès secondary markets remained stable, maintaining values.

Designed by Sir David Chipperfield with interiors by Joseph Dirand, the property features eight restaurants and bars including **Carbone's first European outpost**. Rosewood expanded further with Amsterdam's Palace of Justice conversion (134 rooms overlooking UNESCO-listed canals) and continued Asian growth.

Capella Taipei debuted in 2025 with 86 rooms designed by André Fu, bringing ultra-luxury to Taiwan's capital. **Park Hyatt opened in Kuala Lumpur** on the top 17 floors of the PNB 118 tower, one of Southeast Asia's tallest skyscrapers, with 232 rooms and sweeping Stadium Merdeka views. Four Seasons launched in Mykonos with 94 rooms along Kalo Livadi Bay, while **Aman Rosa Alpina** transforms the historic 1939 Dolomites property (opening late 2025), reducing rooms from 70 to 51 for enhanced space and retaining its three Michelin stars.

Most intriguingly, **Orient Express opened La Minerva in Rome**—the legendary train brand's first hotel—with 93 rooms in a 17th-century residence near the Pantheon, featuring rooftop bar with Pantheon views. Park Hyatt Los Cabos marked the brand's first Mexican resort with 163 ocean-view rooms plus 19 villas at exclusive Cabo del Sol.

Gallery openings signal strategic positioning by blue-chip dealers. **Perrotin opened at Claridge's** in Mayfair, securing 3,800 square feet within the legendary five-star hotel. **Thaddaeus Ropac launched Milan** operations at Palazzo Belgioioso (designed by Giuseppe Piermarini) with two palatial rooms extending into Piazza Belgioioso for sculptures. Major institutional reopenings include **The Frick Collection in April 2025** after Selldorf Architects renovation, the **Studio Museum in Harlem's fall return** in its first purpose-built facility by Adjaye Associates, and the New Museum's expansion by OMA.

High-end restaurant openings concentrate heavily in Los Angeles and New York. **Lielle brought Marcus Jernmark** (former executive chef of Three Michelin-Star Frántzen Stockholm) to LA's Beverlywood with Nordic-rooted cuisine using California ingredients.

Sushi Mekumi opened its NYC location in Hudson Square, bringing two Michelin stars from Kanazawa (2016, 2021) with a 10-seat counter. **Odo launched an East Village kaiseki izakaya**—a more accessible concept from the Two Michelin-Starred chef—featuring 22 seats and entirely gluten-free rice-focused dishes.

Daniel Boulud opened La Tête d'Or, his first-ever steakhouse in the Flatiron District, while **Michael Mina partnered with Steph Curry** for Bourbon Steak at San Francisco's Westin St. Francis. London's JKS Restaurants opened **Ambassador's Clubhouse in NoHo** (8,000 square feet, 175 seats), bringing opulent Punjabi cuisine from their year-old Mayfair location. Notably, **Lilo in Carlsbad earned a Michelin star June 25, 2025**—remarkably fast recognition after opening just April 17.

Watch market shifts toward independents and precious metals

The luxury watch market stabilised in 2025 after pandemic volatility, reaching **$53.69-$59.97 billion** with projections of $134.53 billion by 2032. The tumultuous speculation period ended, with genuine collectors replacing flippers. **Patek Philippe emerged as 2025's standout**, experiencing 50% sales increase versus prior year, with its Complications collection more than doubling sales. The brand raised retail prices 6.8% in May 2025, with the **Aquanaut 5167A now $25,958**, trading at double retail on secondary markets.

Independent watchmakers gained unprecedented traction, often outperforming

ABOVE: Karuizawa 50 Year Old Cask #5132, 1963. 1 Bottle (70cl) per lot. Sold for HK$250,000 on 11 March 2025 at Christie's Online
OPPOSITE: Rolex Daytona 6239 "Paul Newman" ($17.75 million, 2017, Phillips)

Rolex in year-over-year growth. F.P. Journe's **Sonnerie Souverain sold for $1.754 million** at Phillips New York (December 2024), while **Philippe Dufour's Simplicity reached $685,800**, more than doubling estimates. The **Grande & Petite Sonnerie Sapphire Dial commanded $3.7 million**, topping Phillips' December auction. Other independents like Laurent Ferrier, Kari Voutilainen, and H. Moser & Cie attract serious collectors seeking alternatives to the "Holy Trinity."

Rolex maintains dominance with **550% average appreciation from 2010 to 2025**. The Submariner 116610 appreciated 335%, the GMT-Master II gained 506%, and steel Daytonas trade at **$37,096**— However, Oyster Perpetual coloured dials (Tiffany Blue, Coral Red) command $8,000+ secondary prices versus $5,900 retail—when obtainable. The challenge: desirable models remain unavailable at authorised dealers.

Market shifts favor **precious metals over stainless steel** after years of steel dominance. White gold, rose gold, and platinum gain traction as collectors seek exclusivity beyond steel sports models.

> Independent watchmakers gained unprecedented traction, often outperforming Rolex in year-over-year growth.

The **Rolex Daytona 126506 in platinum with ice blue dial** trades at $95,000-$110,000, while Audemars Piguet gold models increased approximately 10% in 2025. Smaller case sizes trend downward from 42mm+ toward 36-39mm, with Tudor and Cartier thriving in this sweet spot.

Dial colours evolved dramatically: **blue dials surged 25% year-over-year** for Omega, now comprising ~15% of sales. Black dials dominate at ~30%, while green dials sustain enthusiasm (Rolex Datejust, Patek Nautilus). Stone dials—malachite, lapis lazuli, tiger's eye—stage comebacks, led by Piaget's Andy Warhol watch. Complications return to favor: annual calendars, chronographs, and GMT functions attract buyers wanting mechanical and aesthetic complexity.

For $10,000, serious collecting begins with the Omega Speedmaster Professional (~$7,000), Rolex Oyster Perpetual 41 ($7,500-$8,000 secondary), Tudor Black Bay 58 (~$3,800-$4,200), Zenith Chronomaster Original (~$8,200), or Cartier Santos Medium ($7,500). **At $50,000**, options include Rolex Daytona steel (~$37,000-$40,000 secondary), Audemars Piguet Royal Oak 15400ST ($36,000-$45,000 pre-owned), Patek Philippe Calatrava in gold ($35,000-$45,000), or Vacheron Constantin

LUXURY INTELLIGENCE | *Market*

ABOVE: Rolex, Seamaster (blue dial). 2025 model.

Overseas Dual Time (~$40,000-$48,000). **At $100,000**, buyers access Patek Nautilus 5726A Annual Calendar ($80,000-$95,000 pre-owned), Rolex Daytona platinum with ice blue dial ($95,000-$110,000), or rare F.P. Journe pieces ($90,000-$120,000 when available).

Beginners should start with Tudor Black Bay 58, Omega Speedmaster, or Grand Seiko in the $3,000-$7,000 range, prioritizing versatility and established brands. Avoid buying purely for investment, chasing hype, or trusting unfamiliar sellers. Pre-owned purchases from reputable dealers like Bob's Watches, SwissWatchExpo, or Hodinkee Shop save 20-40% while already depreciated. Budget for servicing every 5-7 years ($500-$1,500+) and insurance ($100-$300 annually).

Wine market bottoming creates compelling entry points

Fine wine presents one of 2025's most attractive collecting opportunities. The **Liv-ex Fine Wine 100 fell 4.4% in H1 2025 to 311.6**, yet bid-to-offer ratios rose to 0.7—the highest since April 2023—signaling market bottom. Trade volumes jumped 11.9% versus H2 2024 despite price declines, indicating genuine collector demand. After significant 2023-2024 corrections, **market participants agree prices approach floor levels**, creating compelling buying opportunities for cellar replenishment.

Burgundy dominates the fine wine hierarchy, accounting for **68.75% of wines in Liv-ex's highest-value First Tier** (33 of 48

Dial colours evolved dramatically: blue dials surged 25% year-over-year for Omega, now comprising ~15% of sales. Black dials dominate at ~30%, while green dials sustain enthusiasm (Rolex Datejust, Patek Nautilus).

---

wines). **DRC Romanée-Conti averages £172,461 per bottle**, La Tâche £45,061, and Richebourg £31,960. Blue-chip Burgundy Grand Crus remain expensive yet lower than 2022-2023 peaks—opportunistic buyers actively replenish cellars. Domaine Leroy Richebourg 2015 surged **90% since June 2024** to $29,893, while Coche-Dury Corton-Charlemagne 2014 (white Burgundy icon) appreciated 53% since 2020 to $8,438.

Bordeaux struggles with recent vintage overpricing. The 2020-2024 releases at unrealistic En Primeur prices now trade below release, but **2021 vintages find strong demand at corrected prices**: Château Lafite 2021 trades at £3,800 versus £5,800 release. First Growths maintain stability at £4,500-31,000 range. The **2023 Bordeaux vintage offers compelling value**: Château de Fieuzal $28 (92 points), Château Barde-Haut $35 (94 points). Mature vintages (2009-2010) from top châteaux trade near floor prices after corrections.

Italy's **SuperTuscans show 10.4% YTD appreciation**. Sassicaia 2016 climbed 74% since 2020 to $526. The SuperTuscans category declined only 1.3% versus Piedmont's 5.6% drop (hurt by U.S. tariff uncertainty). Vega Sicilia Unico ranked #1 in Liv-ex Power 100 2024 at $544 (97 points, +7% growth). Rhône Valley remains undervalued: M. Chapoutier Ermitage Le Pavillon 2008 surged 40% YTD (£917 - £1,271), while Laurent Charvin Châteauneuf-du-Pape delivers 8-12% annual returns at $50-70.

LUXURY INTELLIGENCE | *Market*

ABOVE: Chateau Lafite Rothschild Bordeaux, France

California cult wines outperform Bordeaux. **Screaming Eagle trades at $3,842-7,000+** per bottle (1992 vintage now $7,000+), with only 400-800 cases produced annually and 13% gains. Harlan Estate commands $1,570 (97 points), while Opus One 2021 trades at $361. Champagne shows resilience: the Champagne 50 index returned to 2020 levels, creating entry opportunities. **Dom Pérignon 1996 P2 Rosé appreciated 62% since 2020** to $1,483. Wine collecting entry points accommodate diverse budgets. **For $50-500**, focus on drinking inventory plus aging potential: Bordeaux value plays like Château de Fieuzal 2023 ($28, 92 points), Laurent Charvin Châteauneuf-du-Pape ($50-70), generic Bourgogne from quality producers ($50-80), and grower Champagnes ($60-150). **For $500-2,000**, serious investment-grade wines emerge: Burgundy Premier & Grand Cru ($150-250), Bordeaux Second Growths ($150-400), Dom Pérignon Vintage ($250-400), Sassicaia 2016 ($526), and Harlan Estate ($1,570). **Above $2,000**, wealth preservation dominates: DRC Romanée-Conti (£172,461), Château Latour (£5,070), Screaming Eagle ($3,842-7,000+), and Château Pétrus (£31,124).

Beginners should start with **Bordeaux for accessibility**—large production, consistent quality, well-documented vintages, with Second Growths at $30-150 entry points. Napa Valley offers New World approachability with well-known producers (Stag's Leap, Caymus) at $50-200. Rhône Valley provides better value than Burgundy/Bordeaux. Avoid Burgundy initially—too complex, expensive, and fragmented until you understand terroir. Current good values include Bordeaux 2021-2023 corrected vintages, mature 2009-2010 Bordeaux near support levels, consistently undervalued Rhône, and grower Champagnes.

Storage costs range from **wine refrigerators ($300-3,500 one-time, $10-30/month electricity)** for under 100 bottles, to climate-controlled self-storage ($50-250/month), to professional wine storage ($2-4 per case monthly). Professional facilities offer perfect conditions, insurance, provenance documentation, and selling services. For collections under $5,000, use home refrigerators; $5,000-$25,000 warrants self-storage; $25,000+ justifies professional facilities. Always factor insurance at 0.5-2% of collection value annually.

Art and automotive markets show selective strength amid broader corrections

The global art market recorded **$57.5 billion in 2024** (down 12% year-over-year), yet transaction volumes grew 3%, indicating market consolidation toward lower price segments. Spring 2025 auctions totaled $1.27 billion, with **72% of collectors drawn to emerging artists**. Market sentiment reached a three-year high, with 52% predicting improvement and **83.9% sell-through rates**—the highest since 2021—demonstrating genuine collector confidence despite headline declines.

Emerging artists achieved breakthrough results. **Yu Nishimura (Japanese painter) set a $406,400 record** for «across the place» (2023), quadrupling the $70,000 estimate, earning David Zwirner representation. **Louis Fratino's "You and Your Things" (2022) reached $756,000**, while **Emma McIntyre's "Up bubbles her amorous breath" (2021) hit $201,600**, doubling estimates. Women Surrealists surge: **Marlene Dumas set the record for living woman artist at $13.65 million** for «Miss January» (1999), Remedios Varo's "Revelación" (1955) brought $6.22 million, and Dorothea Tanning's "Endgame" (1944) exceeded estimates at $2.34 million. Surrealist works above $1 million increased to 20.4% from 9.9% in 2018.

41

LUXURY INTELLIGENCE | *Market*

Figurative painting dominates contemporary trends, alongside oversized abstracts and bold geometry. The **emerging market under $200,000 moves fast**, with 61% of collectors considering works under $5,000. Female artists now represent 44% of HNWI collections and 41% of gallery representation (up 6% from 2018). However, challenges persist: the ultra-contemporary market fell 37.9% between 2023-2024, and major galleries including Blum, Venus Over Manhattan, Kasmin, and CLEARING closed in 2025.

Pricing tiers span dramatically. **Emerging artists ($5K-$50K)** offer entry points for prints, editions, and small originals from gallery-represented artists. **Mid-career ($50K-$500K)** includes established emerging artists like Louis Fratino ($600K-$800K) and Carroll Dunham ($250K-$350K range, exceeded to $762K). **Established artists ($500K+)** feature blue-chip contemporaries like Basquiat ($10M-$25M) and masters like Mondrian ($40M+ for major works, with spring's top lot at $47.56 million).

Beginners should start with galleries rather than auctions for personal guidance and payment plans. Focus on emerging artists with quality gallery representation (David Zwirner, Gagosian, White Cube indicate vetting), strong exhibition history (group shows, solo shows museum exhibitions), and institutional recognition. Use online platforms like Artsy and Saatchi Art for transparency. Avoid buying solely for investment without personal connection, overhyped artists with weak institutional support, or artists with rapidly fluctuating prices.

The classic car market reached **$77.8 billion projected by 2032** (8.7% CAGR), though 2025 shows cooling. The Hagerty Market Rating hit 60.39—lowest since November 2020—with average dealer asking prices at $44,701 (down 9% from 2023's $49,044 peak) and median auction prices at $27,500 (down 20% from 2022). Vehicles sit longer on lots than any time in seven years.

LUXURY INTELLIGENCE | *Market*

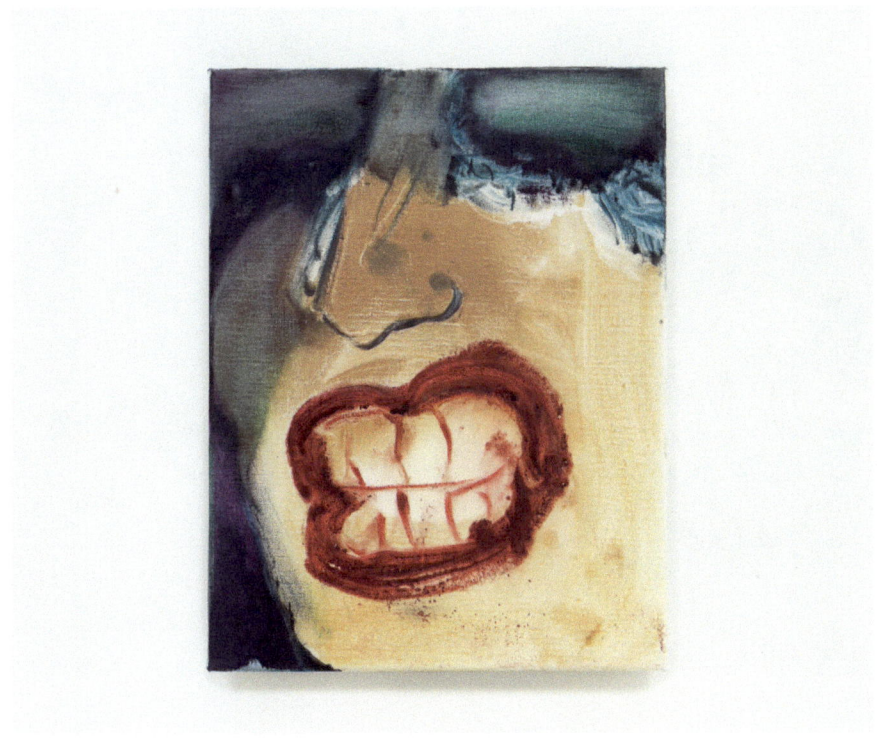

ABOVE: Marlene Dumas, Teeth (2018). Photo David Zwirner Gallery, USA
OPPOSITE: Screaming Eagle Wine

> The overarching trend: genuine collectors replacing speculators, premiumisation across categories, and younger buyers under 40 driving 60% of transactions.

This cooling creates buying opportunities for patient collectors entering at more reasonable valuations.

Japanese classics lead appreciation, with legal imports of 1980s-1990s models driving demand. The **Honda S2000 averages $33,142** (above original MSRP), **Toyota AE86 Corolla hit $22,827** (up from $2,850 in 2021), and **Mazda RX-7 FD Spirit Rs** command extreme prices. The Mazda Miata NA (1990-97) approaches $50,000 for excellent examples, while Nissan Skyline GT-R R32-R34 «Godzilla» series and Honda NSX continue appreciating. SUV collectables surge: early Ford Broncos offer best appreciation bets, while Toyota Land Cruiser FJ40s represent the most sought-after classic SUV.

Modern classics (2000s-2010s) gain recognition. **Porsche 996 and 997 GT models** appreciate significantly, **BMW E46 M3 manual coupes average $26,581**, and Ferrari 308 GTB/GTS "attainable" Ferraris rise quickly. American muscle shows mixed results: 1968-1972 models slump 5-15%, yet 1973 models trade at 40% of earlier prices with only 15% surviving—a value opportunity.

Collector car pricing spans entry-level **($25K-$75K)** with 1990-97 Mazda Miata ($50K approaching), Toyota AE86 ($22,827), and BMW E36 M3 ($26,581); serious collector cars **($75K-$250K)** including Nissan Skyline GT-R R34 ($150K-$250K), Honda NSX ($80K-$150K), and Porsche 993 Carrera ($80K-$150K); and investment-grade **($250K+)** featuring Ferrari F40 ($1.5M-$3M), Porsche 959 ($1.5M-$2M), and McLaren F1 ($15M-$20M).

Beginners should start with **Japanese classics** (Mazda MX5/Miata NA, Toyota Celica, Datsun 510) for affordability, reliability, and strong parts support, or **American pony cars** (1965-66 Mustang base models) for parts availability and established values. Avoid pre-war cars (declining values), heavily speculated ultra-contemporary (37.9% decline), British cars without documentation, and Italian exotics (expensive, specialised). Always secure indoor climate-controlled storage ($100-$300/month if renting), obtain agreed-value insurance from specialty insurers like Hagerty ($500-$2,000 annually), and budget $1,000-$3,000 annual maintenance for entry-level classics.

Strategic insights for sophisticated collectors

December 2025 represents a pivot point where market fundamentals reassert themselves after years of speculation-driven volatility. The convergence of several factors creates distinct opportunities: wine prices near floor levels with improving bid-to-offer ratios, watch market stabilization attracting genuine enthusiasts over flippers, art market consolidation toward emerging artists providing accessible entry points, and automotive cooling enabling patient collectors to negotiate from strength. Cross-category themes dominate.

LUXURY INTELLIGENCE | *Market*

ABOVE: 1997 Mazda MX5/ Miata. Photo: Evan Klein. Courtesy Hagerty

Scarcity premiums drive values across Japanese whisky (supply constraints until 2031), Hermès bags (engineered exclusivity with eliminated waitlists), air-cooled Porsches (no more production), and independent watchmakers (limited production). **Provenance and authenticity** increasingly separate investment-grade from speculative purchases—professional wine storage documentation, watch papers and boxes, art exhibition history, and automotive matching numbers command significant premiums.

Generational wealth transfer of $84 trillion influences collecting trends, with younger buyers under 40 comprising 60% of pre-owned watch requests and driving different value priorities emphasizing sustainability, digital integration, and experiential luxury over pure status.

The **premiumization trend** spans all categories: consumers buying less volume but dramatically higher quality. This manifests in Japanese whisky aged expressions (up 80%), wine collectors focusing on top 2% of wines driving 80% of trade value, watch buyers shifting to precious metals and complications, and art collectors seeking emerging artists with institutional validation rather than purely trendy names. The principle: «drink/use less but better» reshapes luxury consumption from volume to curation.

Liquidity and transparency improve through technology. Online auction sales account for 70 countries represented at Phillips watch auctions, 50% of sneaker resale revenue, and 18% of art sales (double 2019 levels). Platforms like Chrono24, Liv-ex, Artnet Price Database, and Bring a Trailer provide unprecedented price discovery. Fractional ownership democratises access to blue-chip assets, while art lending (up 14% year-over-year) and watch financing create liquidity alternatives to outright sales.

Market timing favors strategic acquisition. Wine corrections create 5-10 year buying opportunities as collectors replenish cellars at support levels. Watch market stabilization means overpaying for hype diminishes while fair value for independents and precious metals emerges. Art's shift toward affordable works under $200,000 "moving fast" rewards early identification of emerging talent before mid-career premiums. Automotive cooling enables 9% below 2023 peaks with vehicles sitting longer—advantageous for patient negotiators avoiding auction fever. Portfolio construction should balance passion with pragmatism. For watches, a three-piece $10,000 collection might include everyday versatile (Tudor/Rolex Oyster Perpetual at $4,000-$7,000), dress/formal (vintage Omega/Cartier Tank at $2,000-$3,000), and tool/beater (Seiko/Hamilton at $300-$800). For wine, $5,000 starting budgets allocate 30% Bordeaux Second Growths, 20% Napa cult wines, 20% Rhône/Tuscany value plays, 15% Champagne, and 15% emerging regions. For art, focus gallery relationships over auction speculation, prioritise emerging artists with clear institutional trajectories, and buy what you genuinely want to live with.

ABOVE: 1954 Mercedes Benz 300SL Gullwing. Courtesy: ATE Australia

Risk management requires acknowledging category-specific challenges. Japanese whisky retail price increases of 50-125% may limit aspirational buyer access. Hermès annual requirement for purchase history alienates longtime clients. Watch market corrections from 2022 peaks demonstrate speculative excess. Wine tariff uncertainty (U.S. buyers withdrew, Asian demand up 55%) creates geopolitical risk. Art gallery closures signal ecosystem stress despite strong auction results. Automotive Gen Z entry at only 8% suggests demographic uncertainty despite 38% millennial participation. Classic cars require significant carrying costs: storage, insurance, maintenance often exceeding annual appreciation in stable years.

The most sophisticated strategy balances immediate enjoyment with long-term appreciation. Buy Japanese whisky to drink (not just hold), Hermès bags to carry (not vault), watches to wear (not flip), wine to cellar and eventually enjoy (not purely invest), art to display (not store), and cars to drive (not garage). The greatest returns come from categories you understand deeply through genuine passion, not spreadsheet analysis. December 2025's market conditions—stabilised valuations, genuine collector demand, improved transparency, and strategic opportunities—reward knowledgeable enthusiasts who commit to 5-10 year holding periods, maintain proper storage and insurance, diversify across categories and price points, and prioritise quality over quantity. The luxury market increasingly favors connoisseurs over speculators, patience over impulsivity, and relationships over transactions.

> Generational wealth transfer of $84 trillion influences collecting trends, with younger buyers emphasising sustainability, digital integration, and experiential luxury over pure status.

Collecting the Uncollectable

The Rise of Experience-Based Luxury

WORDS | ROBERT BURATTI

LUXURY INTELLIGENCE | *Market*

Ultra-wealthy individuals are abandoning traditional luxury goods for exclusive experiences that money can barely buy, fundamentally reshaping a €1.48 trillion global market. This shift represents more than changing consumer preferences—it's a psychological revolution where the world's most affluent collectors are trading Birkin bags for private space flights and rare art for impossible-to-access cultural experiences.

The numbers tell a compelling story: experience-based luxury grew 5% in 2024 while traditional luxury goods declined 2%, marking the first time in decades that experiences outperformed material luxury. Academic research from Cornell University and UT Austin confirms what the wealthy already know—experiences provide more lasting happiness than possessions, creating memories that appreciate over time rather than depreciate like even the finest luxury goods. This transformation emerged from a perfect storm of generational change, social media influence, and post-pandemic values shifts. Gen Z and Millennials, who will command 70-80% of luxury spending by 2030, view experiences as identity-defining investments rather than frivolous purchases. Meanwhile, ultra-high-net-worth individuals increasingly seek what behavioral economist Thomas Gilovich calls "experiential advantage"—the superior satisfaction that comes from investing in doing rather than having.

The shift from material to experiential luxury isn't merely about changing tastes—it's rooted in fundamental psychological research about what creates lasting human satisfaction. Thomas Gilovich's groundbreaking studies at Cornell University demonstrate that people derive more happiness from experiential purchases than material ones across the entire consumption timeline: before, during, and after the purchase.

The psychological mechanisms driving this preference are profound. Experiences create what researchers call "remembered utility"—positive memories that actually improve over time, while material goods suffer from hedonic adaptation and depreciate in perceived value. Dr. David Dubois from INSEAD, a leading expert on luxury consumer behavior, identifies this as the shift from "conspicuous to inconspicuous consumption" among the ultra-wealthy, where sophisticated cultural experiences signal refined taste more effectively than ostentatious material displays.

This psychological foundation explains why ultra-wealthy individuals increasingly invest in transformative experiences. Rather than accumulating objects, they're curating memories, building cultural capital, and creating stories that become integral to their identity. The research shows that experiences form a bigger part of personal identity than possessions and are less susceptible to social comparisons that can diminish satisfaction with luxury goods.

INSEAD's research reveals that wealthy consumers use experiences to signal sophisticated taste and cultural knowledge rather than raw economic power.

This represents a fundamental shift in how the ultra-affluent create and display social status—from external signaling through possessions to internal satisfaction through meaningful experiences.

The luxury market's metamorphosis toward experiences reflects broader demographic and economic shifts that are reshaping global consumption patterns. The global luxury travel market alone reached $2.51 trillion in 2024, projected to reach $4.83 trillion by 2032 with an 8.56% compound annual growth rate that far exceeds traditional luxury goods.

47

LUXURY INTELLIGENCE | *Market*

IMAGES: (Previous) Mediterrean Yacht Charter, Courtesy StockCake | (Above) Interior of the Britannic Explorer. Courtesy Belmond

The demographic breakdown reveals the driving forces behind this transformation. Ultra-high-net-worth individuals with $30+ million in assets increasingly demand "quiet luxury"—remote destinations, private access, and experiences that can't be replicated. Meanwhile, the broader high-net-worth segment, representing 35% of the luxury travel market with $84 billion in annual spending, prioritises boutique experiences and exotic destinations over traditional luxury purchases.

Regional differences illuminate the global nature of this shift. Asian high-net-worth individuals lead the transformation, with 89% of Indian HNWIs and 72% of broader Asian wealth holders planning to increase luxury travel spending. North America commands 32.2% of the global luxury travel market with average wealth per adult of $593,347, while Europe holds 34.06% of market share despite lower per-capita wealth.

The spending patterns reveal how thoroughly experiences have penetrated luxury consumption. Safari and adventure tourism now capture 33% of the luxury tour market, while culinary travel represents the fastest-growing segment at 9.5% annual growth. More tellingly, 50 million luxury consumers have entirely opted out of traditional luxury goods markets between 2022-2024, redirecting their spending toward experiences.

Today's ultra-exclusive experiences command prices that would have seemed impossible for intangible goods just a decade ago. Space tourism epitomises this new luxury landscape, with Virgin Galactic charging $250,000-$900,000 for 90-minute suborbital flights that provide just 4-6 minutes of weightlessness. Blue Origin's auctions have reached $28 million for single seats, while SpaceX's orbital missions command $41.9-$72 million per passenger.

More accessible but equally exclusive experiences fill the spectrum below space tourism. Private museum tours range from £35 for British Museum after-hours access

LUXURY INTELLIGENCE | *Market*

50 million luxury consumers have entirely opted out of traditional luxury goods markets between 2022-2024, redirecting their spending toward experiences.

to £1,100 for empty Metropolitan Museum experiences. Sir John Soane's Museum offers candlelight tours for £700 plus VAT, providing an intimate experience with Regency-era collections when the museum is closed to the public.

The private performance market reveals how celebrities and artists have adapted to experiential luxury demand. A-list performers command millions for private concerts—Jennifer Lopez performed for 20 guests in Macau, while Beyoncé's private performance at an Indian billionaire's wedding reportedly cost tens of millions. More modest private chef experiences range from $65 per person for cocktail canapés to $245 for five-course meals with Michelin-starred chefs.

Premium concierge services have evolved into comprehensive lifestyle management companies. Sienna Charles requires $100+ million net worth and charges $75,000+ annually for lifestyle management, while Velocity Black offers AI-powered concierge services for $3,100 annually. These services provide access to experiences that truly can't be bought through traditional channels—from private museum access to celebrity meet-and-greets.

Traditional luxury brands have fundamentally reimagined their business models to capture the experiential luxury market. LVMH's Clos19 platform exemplifies this transformation, moving beyond selling wine and spirits to offering experiences like private Antarctic expeditions with champagne tastings. The company's upcoming Louis Vuitton hotel on the Champs-Élysées and 20,000-square-foot LV Dream experiential space demonstrate how luxury brands are creating physical environments for exclusive experiences.

Cartier's digital transformation illustrates how technology enables personalised luxury experiences. The company developed "Set for You" diamond ring apps and in-store technology that allows staff to access global inventory while moving freely with clients, creating bespoke experiences that feel more like personal consultation than traditional retail.

The hospitality sector has become a laboratory for experiential luxury innovation. The Ritz-Carlton's yacht collection combines luxury hospitality with "untethered travel freedom," while Four Seasons offers tile painting with Portuguese artisans and chocolate masterclasses with pastry teams. These experiences create what the industry calls "sensory souvenirs"—memories that appreciate over time rather than physical objects that depreciate.

Luxury brands are also transforming their retail presence into experiential destinations. Gucci opened its first "Gucci Salon" in Los Angeles exclusively for VIP clients, recognizing that the top 2% of luxury customers drive 40% of luxury sales. This careful curation of exclusive experiences reflects the industry's understanding that scarcity and personalization have become more valuable than accessibility.

Social media has created complex dynamics around luxury consumption that favor experiences over material goods. TikTok shows 5.3% average engagement rates versus Instagram's 1.1%, with luxury hashtags generating over 5.4 billion views. More significantly, 65% of TikTok users have made unplanned purchases after platform exposure, but the platform's authenticity premium favors experiences over possessions.

The concept of "social currency" has transformed how wealth is displayed and valued. Research shows that posting a photo from a remote eco-lodge in Bali holds more social currency than carrying a Chanel purse among younger demographics. This shift reflects what social media researchers call the move from "conspicuous consumption" to "cultural capital display"—sophisticated signaling through experiences rather than possessions. The investment value comparison reveals the paradox of experiential luxury. Physical luxury goods maintain strong resale markets—the luxury resale market reached $25.78 billion in 2024, projected to reach $81.81 billion by 2031. Hermès Birkin bags have increased 500% over 35 years, while rare whisky appreciated 280% over the past decade,

LUXURY INTELLIGENCE | *Market*

outperforming the S&P 500.

However, experiences provide different types of returns. Multiple academic studies confirm that experiences provide more lasting happiness than material purchases, creating social capital, cultural knowledge, and personal growth that can't be quantified in traditional investment terms. The wealthy are increasingly recognizing that while a Patek Philippe watch might appreciate financially, a private audience with a renowned artist or explorer provides irreplaceable personal enrichment.

The experience economy is forcing traditional luxury sectors to confront fundamental changes in consumer behavior and preferences. Traditional luxury goods contracted 2% in 2024 while experience-based luxury grew 5%, representing the first time in decades that experiences outperformed material luxury across the board.

Individual sectors show varied responses to this disruption. The luxury watch market maintains strong performance with 40% annual growth in resale markets, while jewelry faces headwinds as consumers become more selective. Fashion and leather goods are experiencing the most significant challenges, with small leather accessories still appealing to Gen Z but larger purchases declining as consumers trade down to premium rather than luxury segments.

The art market faces particular challenges as younger consumers prioritise experiences over ownership. Traditional auction houses and galleries are adapting by offering private viewing experiences, artist collaborations, and cultural immersion programs that provide access to artistic creation rather than just acquisition.

Luxury automotive brands have found middle ground by creating experience-based offerings around their products. BMW's real-size AR car configurations and exclusive driving experiences maintain product sales while providing the experiential elements that younger consumers demand. Private aviation has benefited from the shift, with 42% of high-net-worth individuals maintaining or increasing spending on private flights as the ultimate time-saving luxury experience.

Collecting Experiences

The experience economy in luxury is poised for continued evolution driven by technological innovation and demographic change. AI integration is becoming essential for creating personalised experiences at scale, with luxury brands using machine learning to predict preferences and create bespoke offerings. Louis Vuitton's virtual advisors process 60% of customer requests 24/7, while Cartier's

---

Space tourism epitomises this new luxury landscape, with Virgin Galactic charging $250,000-$900,000 for 90-minute suborbital flights that provide just 4-6 minutes of weightlessness.

---

experience data platforms enable rapid digital tool deployment.

The luxury wellness market is expanding beyond traditional spa experiences to include personalised health and longevity programs, biohacking services, and mental health coaching. Space tourism will likely become more accessible, with SpaceX's Starship potentially offering $100,000 tickets for 100 passengers, democratizing what is currently ultra-exclusive.

The metaverse and Web3 technologies are creating entirely new categories of luxury experiences. Louis Vuitton's League of Legends virtual collection and Dolce & Gabbana's €6 million+ NFT sales demonstrate how digital experiences can command premium prices. These virtual luxury goods combine the exclusivity of traditional luxury with the experiential nature of digital consumption.

Sustainability is becoming a competitive necessity rather than optional consideration. 75% of luxury travellers prioritise sustainable options, and emerging regulations require environmental transparency that favors experiences over resource-intensive manufactured goods. This trend suggests that experience-based luxury aligns with broader environmental consciousness among affluent consumers.

The transformation of luxury consumption from material goods to exclusive experiences represents more than a market trend—it's a fundamental shift in how the world's wealthiest individuals define value, status, and personal fulfillment. The convergence of psychological research, demographic change, and technological capability has created a perfect storm favoring experiences over possessions among those with the means to choose either.

This evolution challenges traditional notions of luxury while creating unprecedented opportunities for brands, service providers, and experience creators. The ultra-wealthy are increasingly becoming patrons of impossibility—funding and participating in experiences that push the boundaries of what money can buy. From private space flights to exclusive cultural access, they're collecting memories and capabilities rather than objects and possessions.

The implications extend beyond luxury markets to broader questions about value creation in an experience economy. As the generation that will command 70-80% of luxury spending by 2030 prioritises experiences over possessions, traditional luxury brands must either adapt or risk obsolescence. The future belongs to those who can create, curate, and deliver experiences that transform rather than merely satisfy—turning luxury from something you own into something you become.

IMAGE: Artist's illustration of Space Perspective's Spaceship Neptune high above Earth. Courtesy: Space Perspective

LUXURY INTELLIGENCE | *Market*

Couture Capital

Why Fashion Has Become the Investment You Can Wear

WORDS | **ELLA TOMLIN**

In the rarefied world of collecting, where vintage Rolexes and first-growth Bordeaux have long reigned supreme, a quiet revolution is unfolding. High-end fashion collecting—once dismissed as frivolous or fleeting has emerged as one of the most sophisticated and lucrative pursuits in the luxury market. And make no mistake: this is very much a thing today.

The preloved clothing market already accounts for £175 billion, representing 9% of total global fashion sales, with a continuous upwards trajectory. Yet this isn't simply about buying secondhand clothes. What's happening represents a fundamental shift in how discerning collectors view fashion: not as disposable consumption, but as wearable art, cultural artefacts, and genuine investment vehicles.

Certain designer pieces have demonstrated remarkable appreciation, with Dior and Prada resale values increasing by 12% and 11% respectively over the past five years. But the real story isn't merely financial—it's about the emergence of fashion as a recognised artistic discipline worthy of serious collecting.

Museums and major institutions are increasingly building fashion collections, having come to recognise fashion design as an artistic discipline worthy of archiving. The Metropolitan Museum of Art's blockbuster Alexander McQueen retrospective wasn't just entertainment; it was validation. When museums compete for the same pieces as private collectors, you know the market has matured.

Consider the legendary pieces now commanding auction house attention: An Yves Saint Laurent Mondrian block dress—inspired by Piet Mondrian's geometric works—commands prices upwards of $20,000 at auction, coveted by collectors and museums alike. These aren't clothes; they're historical documents, artistic statements, and increasingly, appreciating assets.

Today's fashion collecting spans multiple categories, each with its own sophisticated following.

LUXURY INTELLIGENCE | *Market*

Archive Fashion: Pieces from specific designers and eras are experiencing particular demand—Phoebe Philo's Céline (2008-2017), Nicolas Ghesquière's Balenciaga (1997-2021), and John Galliano's Dior (1996-2011) represent the holy grails of contemporary fashion collecting. These aren't random preferences; they're informed by an understanding of pivotal moments when visionary designers fundamentally altered how we dress.

Y2K Revival: Demand for Prada's Crystal Re-Edition 2000 mini bag increased by 1,344% year-over-year, whilst pieces from Miu Miu's SS05 collection remain particularly coveted. This isn't mere nostalgia—it's a recognition that certain moments in fashion history produced work of enduring relevance.

Couture Rarities: For those with deeper pockets and scholarly inclinations, Elsa Schiaparelli's Surrealist pieces from the 1920s onwards—including lobster handbags and trompe l'oeil suits—remain extremely rare and sought-after by museums and collectors, with examples like her Zodiac jacket from 1938-39 realising £100,000 at auction.

The Knowledge Game

What separates genuine collectors from casual buyers? Expertise. The serious fashion collector operates with the same rigour as those pursuing Old Master paintings or rare manuscripts.

Fashion houses like Chanel and Louis Vuitton have distinct authenticity indicators that evolve over time, whilst material quality, construction methods, and hardware details help identify genuine vintage pieces. Professional authentication services have become essential, particularly for high-value acquisitions. The due diligence required isn't trivial—it's a testament to the market's maturity.

Provenance matters enormously. Items worn by style icons or captured by important photographers carry significant premiums for collectors. A Chanel jacket is valuable; the same jacket worn by Princess Diana might be worth 100 times more. This isn't irrational—it's understanding that fashion exists at the intersection of craft, culture, and personal narrative.

Beyond Mere Possession

Leading collectors emphasise that they're not just collecting historical fashion and vintage, but curating a narrative of power, elegance, and defiance through what they wear—the opposite of mainstream or fast fashion. This philosophical approach distinguishes true

---

> Demand for Prada's Crystal Re-Edition 2000 mini bag increased by 1,344% year-over-year, whilst pieces from Miu Miu's SS05 collection remain particularly coveted.

---

connoisseurs from those simply chasing trends.

There's also something profoundly satisfying about wearing fashion history. In an increasingly digital world, there's something wildly refreshing about wearing fashion that has existed for more than 100 years. A Victorian blouse or Edwardian lace carries stories and craftsmanship that simply cannot be replicated by contemporary production.

Search interest in luxury fashion surged notably in late 2024 and early 2025, with distinct peaks aligning with seasonal demand, whilst the resale market has become increasingly sophisticated with platforms like The RealReal and Vestiaire Collective. Major fashion houses are no longer threatened by the secondary market—they're embracing it. Brands like Banana Republic, Mulberry, and others are now releasing vintage capsules and reissues, whilst some are even selling original archival pieces directly.

This institutional endorsement matters. When Hermès or Chanel acknowledges the value of their vintage pieces, they're validating what collectors have known all along: truly exceptional fashion transcends its moment.

There's now recognition that even some major designer names have slipped on quality, and that it's better to buy 'old' over new. This isn't romanticism—it's pragmatism. The craftsmanship in a 1980s Chanel suit often surpasses what's produced today, even at eye-watering price points.

Contemporary luxury fashion emphasises craftsmanship sitting at the forefront, with intricate embroidery, artisanal textures, and handmade details distinguishing true luxury from high street alternatives. Yet collectors know that this emphasis on craft isn't new—it's a return to standards that vintage pieces already embody.

Building a Collection

For those considering entering this world, several principles emerge from established collectors:

Start with knowledge, not acquisition. Study designers, understand movements, learn to recognise quality and authenticity. Visit museums, read extensively, handle pieces whenever possible.

Focus and specialise. The most successful collectors develop deep expertise in specific designers, eras, or aesthetics rather than accumulating randomly.

Condition and provenance are paramount. Original packaging, tags, and accessories significantly impact value, whilst

LUXURY INTELLIGENCE | *Market*

ABOVE: Prada Re-Edition 2005 mini crystal-studded satin bag. Courtesy: Prada

understanding condition grading—terms like "mint," "excellent," and "fair"—helps collectors make informed decisions.

Think long-term. Fashion collecting represents "a fashion for collecting fashion," underpinned by major brands finally embracing the secondary market rather than feeling threatened by it. This legitimisation creates a stable foundation for values to appreciate over decades, not just seasons.

The Future Landscape

The fashion collecting market in 2025 shows no signs of slowing. By 2025, the pre-owned luxury market is projected to reach $30 billion, highlighting growing consumer interest in sustainable luxury and collectible pieces. But sustainability is only part of the story. What's driving growth is a genuine appreciation for fashion as cultural artefact and investment vehicle. We're witnessing the mainstreaming of what was once a niche pursuit. Designers like Daniel Roseberry are incorporating antique ribbons from Parisian shops into Schiaparelli's couture collections, whilst Valentino and Simone Rocha reference Victorian and Renaissance eras. When contemporary designers pay homage to fashion history in this manner, they're acknowledging what collectors already know: the archive is alive, relevant, and infinitely inspiring.

High-end fashion collecting isn't for everyone, nor should it be. It requires capital, certainly, but more importantly it demands knowledge, passion, and a particular sensibility—the same qualities that distinguish serious collectors in any field. Those who approach it seriously discover something remarkable: a world where artistry, history, and personal expression converge. Where a 1960s Courrèges coat isn't merely clothing but a statement about optimism and the Space Age. Where a vintage Hermès Kelly bag carries the patina of decades and stories untold.

The question isn't whether high-end fashion collecting is "a thing today"—clearly, it is. The question is whether you possess the connoisseurship to participate meaningfully in this rarefied world. Because in the end, that's what separates collectors from consumers: the ability to recognise not just what something costs, but what it's truly worth.

ABOVE: Christian Dior, Paris couture house, est. 1947. John Galliano, designer since 1996. Gibraltarian, born 1960, emigrated to England 1966, worked in France 1990– Dress, hat and boots, no. 39 designed 2000 (front view). Spring–summer, made 2003 silk, paint, lacquer, metal, leather, couture no. 333 381 (a) 224.2 cm (centre back); 35.0 cm (waist, flat) (dress); (b) 31.0 cm (height); 58.0 cm (width) (hat); (c–d) 51.8 x 8.2 x 21.2 cm each (boots) National Gallery of Victoria, Melbourne
OPPOSITE: The first Birkin handbag sold for a staggering 8.6 million euros in Paris to become the second most valuable fashion item ever sold at auction. Courtesy: Sothebys.

LUXURY INTELLIGENCE | *Market*

LUXURY INTELLIGENCE | *Market*

TAG Heuer's Best-Kept Secret

Why the TAG Heuer 2000 Series Deserves Serious Collector Attention

WORDS | **ROBERT BURATTI**

TAG Heuer's longest-running model defined a generation of tool-watch collecting. Its absence from the brand's heritage narrative creates the decade's most compelling horological arbitrage opportunity. The watch that defined accessible luxury sports horology for two decades remains curiously undervalued

The watch collecting world has a peculiar habit of overlooking the obvious. Whilst enthusiasts chase the heritage glamour of Carreras and the Monaco's cinematic cachet, the TAG Heuer 2000 Series—the brand's longest-running model family and the direct ancestor of today's Aquaracer—languishes in relative obscurity. This represents not a failure of the watch, but rather a failure of imagination amongst collectors.

Consider the facts dispassionately. The 2000 Series survived 22 years in continuous production (1982-2004) before evolving into the Aquaracer line. Were it not for a marketing department's whim to rebrand in the mid-2000s, we'd be celebrating over 40 years of the 2000 Series this year. No other TAG Heuer collection can claim such longevity—not even the vaunted Carrera, which spent decades in hibernation before its resurrection.

Yet TAG Heuer itself seems almost embarrassed by this achievement. The 2000 Series isn't considered 'Heritage'. There's no anniversary edition, no retrospective catalogue, no museum display. This institutional amnesia creates an intriguing arbitrage opportunity for the discerning collector: significant watches, historically important watches, available at prices that would make a Submariner collector weep with envy.

Honesty compels us to acknowledge that the 2000 Series didn't emerge fully formed like Athena from Zeus's head. The 1982 launch models are, to be charitable, of their time. Ball bearing-adorned bezels. 'HEUER 2000' printed in a font that belongs on a 1970s science fiction paperback. Mustard yellow straps that would make even the most committed period enthusiast wince.

These early experiments are so rare in the wild that one suspects even their original purchasers quickly reconsidered their choices.

LUXURY INTELLIGENCE | *Market*

Finding a 944.006—that white-dialled, gold-bezelled curiosity on its unfortunate mustard strap—would be genuinely noteworthy, if only as a cautionary tale about the perils of trend-chasing in watch design.

Finding Its Voice

The series took several years to settle into its identity, with various 'interesting' diversions along the way. The Tri-Star sub-collection, launched in 1987, represents one such evolutionary dead end—competent watches, certainly, but lacking the focused purpose that would eventually define the line's appeal. By the early 1990s, however, the formula crystallised: robust dive-watch construction, legible dials, rotating bezels with proper dive-watch functionality, and pricing that made serious tool-watch capability accessible to professionals who weren't investment bankers. This was the 2000 Series at its finest—unpretentious, functional, and honestly priced.

> The same forces driving Speedmaster and Explorer prices skyward will eventually discover that 22 years of continuous production created depth in the vintage market without destroying collectability.

The Collectible Golden Era

The mid-to-late 1990s represent the sweet spot for collectors. The 1996-1997 models achieved a design maturity that still looks purposeful today. The WK1110 through WK1121 references established clean, legible aesthetics. The introduction of the 2000 Sports variants (WM-series references) added versatility without compromising the core collection's identity.

Then came the special editions. The various Grand Prix limited editions—Malaysian, Australian, Monaco, Silverstone—offer focused collecting opportunities. These weren't cynical marketing exercises churning out endless 'limited' variants; they were genuinely scarce pieces tied to TAG Heuer's motorsport heritage.

More intriguing still are the truly rare variants: the Jordanian Royal Family crest dial (WK111D), the Mild Seven special edition, the Stadium Australia limited edition, even the delightfully incongruous Mickey Mouse Sports model (WM1112.BA0317DI). These pieces offer the dual pleasures of rarity and narrative—always more interesting than mere scarcity.

Market dynamics offer their own form of validation. Whilst you can still acquire solid 2000 Series examples for $600-1,000, try finding a red-dial model for under $1,400. The market has spoken: certain variants command premiums that reflect genuine collector demand rather than speculative froth.

The 1997 CK2112 red-dial chronograph represents the apotheosis of this trend. Here was the 2000 Series at its most confident: bold colour choice, integrated chronograph functionality, and an aesthetic that managed to be both sporty and refined. Good examples now command prices that seem modest only in comparison to the broader luxury watch market's inflation—but represent genuine value compared to acquiring equivalent functionality in a 'heritage' piece.

The range's final flourish deserves particular attention. The 2002 WK111A Multigraph—with its digital-analogue hybrid display—represented TAG Heuer's attempt to drag the 2000 Series into the 21st century. Whether this succeeded aesthetically remains debatable (the digital display has a certain retro-futuristic charm, though 'charm' may be generous). What's undeniable is its rarity and its role as the series' swan song.

The Collecting Case

Why collect the 2000 Series? Not for investment returns—if that's your priority, buy property or index funds. Collect it because it represents an honest era in watchmaking, before 'accessible luxury' became an oxymoron, when a company could produce genuinely capable tool watches without needing to justify their existence through manufactured heritage narratives.

Collect it because the market hasn't caught up yet. The same forces driving Speedmaster and Explorer prices skyward will eventually discover that 22 years of continuous production created depth in the vintage market without destroying collectability. Scarcity matters, but so does significance.

Collect it because wearing a well-maintained WK1113—that gorgeous blue-dial variant on bracelet—generates a particular satisfaction: the knowledge that you're wearing a genuinely capable watch that cost less than a mediocre dinner for two, whilst others are queuing for the privilege of overpaying for the current hype piece.

The 2000 Series will never be the Monaco. It lacks that model's cinematic pedigree and design audacity. It will never command Carrera prices, absent that nameplate's racing romanticism. This is precisely the point.

Serious collecting isn't about chasing the same references everyone else desires. It's about recognising quality, significance, and value where others see only the mundane. The TAG Heuer 2000 Series—unloved by its own manufacturer, overlooked by the broader market, yet representing 22 years of continuous refinement—offers exactly this opportunity.

The question isn't whether the 2000 Series deserves collector attention. The question is how long before everyone else works this out.

Finding examples: Specialist dealers like Est1897 occasionally stock well-maintained pieces. eBay remains viable for patient collectors willing to sort through questionable listings. Expect to pay $600-1,000 for standard references in good condition, $1,000-1,600 for desirable variants like the red dial or blue dial models, and $1,400-2,400 for genuine limited editions with documentation.

> Serious collecting isn't about chasing the same references everyone else desires. It's about recognising quality, significance, and value where others see only the mundane

LUXURY INTELLIGENCE | Market

The Case against Compromise

Ferrari 296 Speciale

WORDS | **JAMES MASTER**

A 60-kilogram weight reduction and the most powerful rear-drive Ferrari ever made. On paper, another hypercar arms race. In practice, something rather more interesting.

There's a particular kind of collector who becomes insufferable the moment Ferrari announces a Speciale. You know the type: three Ferraris in the garage already, WhatsApp messages from Maranello before the press release drops, that knowing smile when asked about allocation. They're deeply annoying, of course. They're also, unfortunately, usually right.

The 296 Speciale arrives as Ferrari's latest exercise in making an already exceptional car better in ways that shouldn't matter but absolutely do. It follows a lineage stretching back to 2003's 360 Challenge Stradale—each iteration taking the entry-level mid-engine Ferrari and applying lessons from the track, then charging handsomely for the education. The 430 Scuderia. The 458 Speciale. The 488 Pista. Each became the version collectors actually wanted, regardless of the premium. This one sold out before Ferrari announced it to the public.

But here's where things become complicated: by reusing the Speciale name for the first time since the 458, Ferrari has inadvertently created a direct comparison to what many consider the benchmark—the naturally aspirated V8 car that howled to 9,000 rpm with an intensity bordering on religious experience. The 296 Speciale faces an impossible standard set by its own naming convention.

Does it matter? Perhaps not. As Ferrari's chief marketing officer now explicitly states, cars depreciate—even special-series Ferraris. They should be bought to be driven and loved, first and foremost. Sensible advice that conveniently sidesteps the question of whether this turbocharged V6 hybrid can match the emotional engagement of its predecessor whilst surpassing it in measurable performance. The answer, as it happens, proves more nuanced than the question deserves.

LUXURY INTELLIGENCE | *Market*

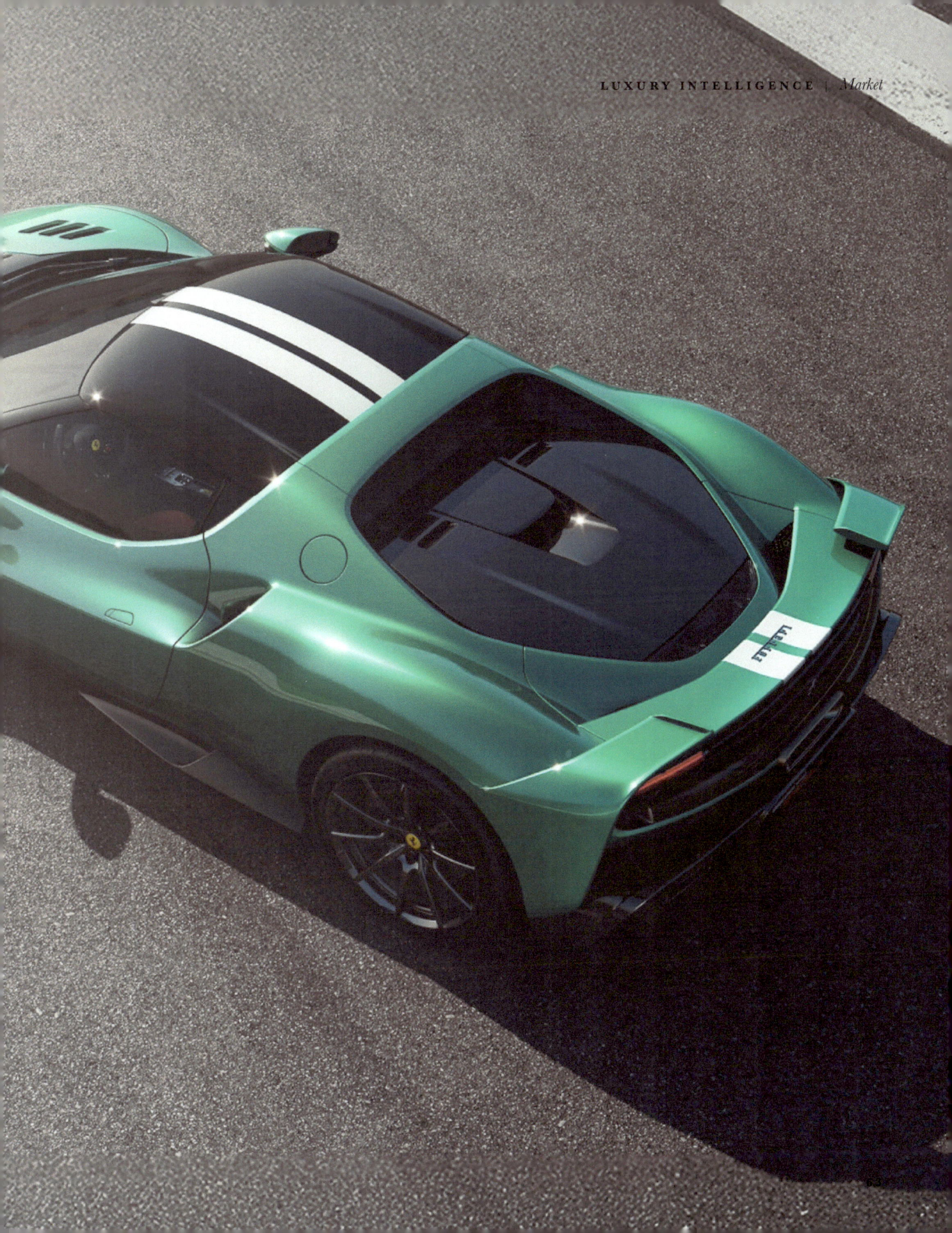

LUXURY INTELLIGENCE

What Makes It Speciale

Let's dispense with the headline figures quickly. The twin-turbocharged 3.0-litre V6 hybrid powertrain now produces 868 horsepower combined—691 from the engine, 178 from the electric motor. That's 49 additional horses over the standard 296 GTB, making this the most powerful rear-wheel-drive production Ferrari in history. It achieves 0-100 km/h in 2.8 seconds and laps Ferrari's Fiorano test circuit in 1:19—two seconds faster than a 296 GTB with the Assetto Fiorano package, equalling the time of the considerably more expensive, all-wheel-drive SF90 Stradale.

Performance statistics that would have been hypercar territory a decade ago. Today, they're merely the entry fee.

What matters more is how Ferrari achieved them. The Speciale sheds 60 kilograms through obsessive attention to component-level weight reduction. Titanium connecting rods borrowed from the multi-million-dollar F80 hypercar. A lightened crankshaft. Excess material machined from the engine block and cylinder heads using techniques from the Le Mans-winning 499P. Titanium fasteners throughout. The engine alone weighs nearly nine kilograms less than standard, accounting for 15 per cent of the total weight saving.

This is not the lazy approach of simply removing sound deadening and calling it "racing character". Every component has been reconsidered. The carbon-fibre door panels are sculpted rather than flat, saving weight whilst maintaining structural rigidity. The speakers eschew conventional grilles in favour of precisely drilled holes in the carbon fibre. Even the shift paddles behind the steering wheel are carbon fibre.

One could argue this level of detail borders on absurdity. One would be missing the point entirely.

The Ferarri 296 Speciale. All images courtesy of Ferrari S.p.A

The Aerodynamics Problem

Ferrari faced an interesting challenge with the 296 Speciale. The standard GTB already generated substantial downforce. Making it significantly more track-capable required not just adding wings and splitters, but fundamentally rethinking how air moved around the car without compromising the elegant silhouette that makes it suitable for actual road use.

The solution demonstrates genuine engineering rather than styling theatre. An "aero damper" vent now sits in the bonnet just before the windscreen, connected to a duct originating at the front splitter. Derived from the 296 Challenge race car, it reduces aerodynamic variability caused by changing ground clearance during braking and compression—the kind of detail that matters enormously at ten-tenths but would never appear in a promotional video.

New brake cooling ducts. Radiator openings 12 per cent larger. "Gamma" winglets sprouting from the rear haunches. An active rear wing with a new intermediate position for situations where maximum downforce isn't required. The result: 435 kilograms of downforce at 250 km/h—20 per cent more than the GTB—whilst maintaining a 330 km/h top speed. The car looks angrier, certainly. More aggressive. But it doesn't look ridiculous, which for a Speciale variant is something of an achievement.

The Hybrid Question

Here we must address the six-cylinder elephant in the room. Ferrari positioning a turbocharged V6 hybrid as a flagship performance model would have been heretical a decade ago. The 458 Speciale's naturally aspirated V8 howled to 9,000 rpm with an intensity that bordered on religious experience. The 296's V6, regardless of how impressive its 234 horsepower per litre specific output might be, cannot match that soundtrack.

This is factually correct and also entirely beside the point. The 296 Speciale's powertrain delivers something different but no less compelling: a perfectly flat torque curve between 3,000 and 7,000 rpm that makes gear selection nearly irrelevant. Shift times reduced by a third through a clever trick where the electric motor delivers a jolt of torque just before each change, filling the traditional power dip. An "extra boost" function in Qualify mode that provides additional electric assistance for corner exit, managed by thermal monitoring to prevent component overload—straight from the SF90 XX Stradale. Ferrari's engineers describe the shift strategy as maximising "driver engagement". Marketing language that, for once, undersells the reality. The upshift doesn't just happen quickly—it arrives with a kick reminiscent of an old GM Turbo-Hydramatic 400 with a shift kit.

> Ferrari's chief marketing officer now explicitly states: cars depreciate—even special-series Ferraris. They should be bought to be driven and loved, first and foremost.

ABOVE: The Ferarri 296 GTB. All images courtesy of Ferrari S.p.A

It feels mechanical, visceral, physical in a way modern dual-clutch gearboxes typically don't. The sound remains less operatic than V8 or V12 predecessors. But opera isn't the only valid art form.

The Collectability Calculation

Let's discuss what everyone's thinking about but nobody wants to say directly: investment potential. The 430 Scuderia from 2009 with 7,425 miles currently commands $429,000 AUD. The later 458 Speciale with similar mileage sits at $722,000-$780,000 AUD, with the Aperta version reaching $1,365,000 AUD. The turbocharged 488 Pista occupies the $546,000-$683,000 AUD range. Pattern recognition suggests the 296 Speciale should follow suit.

The Australian market presents a more challenging proposition. The Speciale starts at AUD $865,569 before on-road costs, with the Aperta at $984,020. However—and Ferrari's own chief marketing officer now says this explicitly—cars depreciate. Even special-series Ferraris. Enrico Galliera's recent comments represent a remarkable shift in messaging: cars should be bought to be driven and loved, first and foremost. This isn't marketing speak. It's a warning.

Regular 296 GTBs already trade below their original pricing in various markets. The Speciale commands a premium of roughly $130,000 over the standard car—you're paying for 60 fewer kilograms, 49 additional horsepower, improved aerodynamics, and exclusivity. With typical options (carbon package, special livery, stripes, personalisation), the actual transaction price approaches one million Australian dollars. Add stamp duty at up to nine per cent depending on state, and you're handing over more than the average house costs in Australia.

Will it hold value? Probably, if maintained carefully with sensible mileage. The engineering substance is genuine rather than cosmetic. Production remains limited though not disclosed. The entire two-year production run sold out before public announcement—a good sign.

Purchase one because you want to drive it. If it appreciates, consider that a pleasant bonus rather than the primary objective.

What Is It Worth?

The 296 Speciale will reach Australian shores during the first quarter of 2026 as a coupé, with the Speciale A convertible following mid-year. Pricing approaches $500,000 USD, with Ferrari absorbing the 25 per cent import tariff rather than passing costs to customers. Australian pricing will likely settle around AUD $750,000-800,000 before inevitable on-road costs and option selections.

For context: that's AUD $130,000 more than a standard 296 GTB. You're paying for 60 fewer kilograms, 49 additional horsepower, substantially improved aerodynamics, and titanium components throughout. Also for exclusivity, naturally. And for membership in that particular club of insufferable collectors who somehow secured allocation.

Is it worth it? Objectively, almost certainly not. The standard 296 GTB already provides more performance than any reasonable person could deploy on public roads. The Speciale's improvements manifest primarily at track-day commitment levels that invite conversations with constabulary or race control, depending on venue.

Subjectively, entirely.

For those fortunate enough to secure allocation, the advice is straightforward: buy it. Drive it. Enjoy it. If it appreciates, consider that a pleasant bonus. If it doesn't, you'll have owned one of the most capable road-legal race cars ever produced. The truly annoying collectors who secured allocation before announcement? They're probably right again. Frustrating, but there it is.

All images courtesy of Ferrari S.p.A

FEATURE

Price of Admission

What it actually costs to start collecting seriously and where your money goes furthest

The question every aspiring collector asks: "How much do I need to start?" The answer depends less on the number than on what you're trying to accomplish. A $10,000 watch collection can be more thoughtfully curated than a $100,000 hodgepodge. Here's what different budget levels buy you across categories—and crucially, where beginners should focus their first dollars.

FEATURE | *The Price of Admission*

FEATURE | *The Price of Admission*

Watches
The Three-Tier Reality

At $10,000

This is where serious watch collecting actually begins. You have three strategic approaches:

The Single Grail

One exceptional piece that does everything. An Omega Speedmaster Professional ($7,000-$8,000) or Rolex Oyster Perpetual 41 in a desirable dial color ($7,500-$8,500 on the pre-owned market) delivers brand heritage, versatility, and genuine collecting credibility. You'll wear it everywhere and never apologise for it.

The Practical Trio
A more versatile approach splits your budget:

Everyday ($4,000-$5,000): Tudor Black Bay 58 or Omega Aqua Terra—appropriate for office or weekend

Dress ($2,500-$3,500): Vintage Omega Seamaster De Ville or Cartier Tank Must—credibility without flash

Beater ($800-$1,500): Seiko Prospex or Hamilton Khaki—something you actually wear hiking or traveling

The Vintage Route
$10,000 buys serious entry into vintage: a 1960s Rolex Datejust, early Omega Constellation, or Jaeger-LeCoultre Reverso. Requires homework but offers character modern pieces can't match.

At $50,000

Now you're accessing the pieces people actually covet.

What's Available:

Rolex Daytona in steel (if you can find one): $37,000-$40,000 secondary market

Audemars Piguet Royal Oak 15400ST: $40,000-$48,000 pre-owned

Patek Philippe Calatrava in gold: $35,000-$45,000

Vacheron Constantin Overseas: $40,000-$48,000

A strong collection of 3-4 pieces: One grail ($25,000-$30,000) plus supporting cast

The Challenge: At this level, you're competing with serious collectors who know exactly what they want. Authorised dealer relationships matter. Pre-owned from reputable dealers (Hodinkee, Crown & Caliber, Bob's Watches) becomes essential.

Where to focus: If you're not passionate about complications or haute horology, this might not be your category. Consider whether that $45,000 Patek brings you more joy than a $15,000 watch plus $30,000 worth of wine or art.

At $100,000

You're now accessing genuine haute horology and investment-grade pieces.

What's Available:

Patek Philippe Nautilus 5726A Annual Calendar: $85,000-$95,000 pre-owned

Rolex Daytona in platinum with ice blue dial: $95,000-$110,000

F.P. Journe Chronomètre Souverain: $90,000-$120,000 (when available)

A.Lange & Söhne Lange 1: $45,000-$65,000

Vacheron Constantin Overseas Perpetual Calendar: $85,000-$95,000

The Reality: At this budget, you're not buying a watch—you're buying access to a world. The conversations, the knowledge, the community. If that doesn't interest you, you're overspending.

Beginner's Don't: Don't start here. Even if you can afford it, buying a $100,000 watch before you've worn a $5,000 piece daily for a year means you don't yet know what you value.

FEATURE | *The Price of Admission*

Where to start:

The Omega Geneve or Seamaster circa 1960s $800-$4,200, leaves room for a second watch, and teaches you what you actually value before committing larger sums.

FEATURE | *The Price of Admission*

Wine
The Patient Investment

At $10,000

A serious entry-level cellar of 150-200 bottles focusing on drinking pleasure with aging potential.

Smart Allocation:

Bordeaux Cru Classé ($3,000): Ten cases of well-priced Second and Third Growth 2016-2021 vintages at $250-$350/case. Ready to drink in 5-10 years.

Burgundy Village-Level ($2,500): Bourgogne Rouge from quality producers (Comte Armand, Hudelot-Noëllat) at $50-$80/bottle. Learn the region without bankrupting yourself.

Napa Cabernet ($2,000): Six cases of established but not-quite-cult producers at $80-$150/bottle. Ridge, Shafer, Heitz deliver now and improve with age.

Rhône Valley ($1,500): Best value in serious French wine. Châteauneuf-du-Pape, Côte-Rôtie, Hermitage from quality producers at $50-$120/bottle.

Champagne ($1,000): Grower Champagnes at $60-$100/bottle. Better quality than big houses, educational, drinkable now.

Storage: Budget $500-$1,000 for a wine refrigerator or $50-$100/month for off-site storage. This isn't optional.

At $50,000

Now you're building an investment-quality cellar of 400-500 bottles with serious aging potential.

Strategic Allocation:

Blue-Chip Bordeaux First Growths ($15,000): Three cases of Lafite, Latour, or Margaux from strong vintages (2015, 2016) at $4,500-$6,000/case

Grand Cru Burgundy ($15,000): Individual bottles of DRC, Rousseau, Roumier from solid vintages at $500-$2,000/bottle

Cult Napa ($10,000): Screaming Eagle, Harlan Estate, Colgin—if you have access. Otherwise, Scarecrow, Continuum, Dalla Valle.

Mature Bordeaux ($5,000): Drinking-ready wines from 2005, 2009, 2010 vintages

Diversification ($5,000): Super Tuscans, Barolo, aged Champagne, Sauternes

The Challenge: At this level, provenance matters enormously. Buy from reputable auction houses (Acker, Sotheby's, Hart Davis Hart) or established merchants with proper storage documentation.

At $100,000

You're now competing for the world's finest bottles and can build a true investment cellar.

What's Available:

DRC Allocation: If you can secure it, a case of DRC wines ($50,000-$80,000)

Mature First Growths: Cases from legendary vintages (1982, 1990, 2000) at $10,000-$25,000/case

Burgundy Icons: Multiple bottles from Domaine Leroy, Rousseau, Roumier across vintages

Vertical Collections: Complete vintage runs of specific châteaux or domaines

The Reality: Professional storage is mandatory ($200-$400/month for this volume). Insurance essential (1-2% of value annually). You need relationships with merchants, auction houses, and possibly sommelier consultants.

Beginner's Don't: Don't buy a $5,000 bottle before you've properly tasted a $500 one. The learning curve is steep and expensive mistakes are permanent.

FEATURE | *The Price of Admission*

Storage:

Budget $500-$1,000 for a wine refrigerator or $50-$100/month for off-site storage.

This isn't optional.

Where to start:

Bordeaux 2021 vintage. Market corrections mean you're buying at reasonable prices, the vintage is strong, and you'll learn proper aging.

FEATURE | *The Price of Admission*

Art
The Relationship Game

At $10,000

You're acquiring works from emerging artists with gallery representation—the foundation of serious collecting.

What's Available:

• Emerging Artist Paintings ($5,000-$8,000): Small to medium works from gallery-represented artists showing in group shows at respected galleries

• Prints & Editions ($1,000-$3,000): Limited edition prints from established mid-career artists

• Photography ($2,000-$5,000): Numbered photographs from recognised photographers

• Works on Paper ($1,500-$4,000): Drawings, watercolors, mixed media from promising artists

Where to Buy:

• Emerging galleries (not blue-chip yet, but professionally run)

• Art fairs' "Positions" or "Discoveries" sections

• Online platforms: Artsy, Saatchi Art for transparency and payment plans

• Directly from artist studios (if you've done serious research)

At $50,000

You're accessing mid-career artists and can begin building a cohesive collection.

What's Available:

• Mid-Career Paintings ($20,000-$40,000): Substantial works from artists with museum exhibitions and strong secondary market presence

• Emerging Blue-Chip ($15,000-$30,000): Works from artists represented by major galleries (Gagosian, Hauser & Wirth, David Zwirner) before they hit $100,000+ levels

• Sculpture ($10,000-$25,000): Serious three-dimensional works from recognised artists

• Photography ($5,000-$15,000): Important prints from established photographers

Strategic Approach: Build a collection of 3-5 works around a theme: figuration, abstraction, a particular region, or a specific art movement. Cohesion increases both intellectual and market value.

Where to focus: Develop relationships with 2-3 galleries. Attend openings, express genuine interest, be a known presence. Access to best works comes through relationships, not money alone.

At $100,000

You can acquire museum-quality works and compete for attention from major galleries.

What's Available:

• Established Contemporary ($50,000-$80,000): Works from artists with major museum retrospectives and strong auction records

• Blue-Chip Emerging ($30,000-$50,000): The absolute best works from hottest emerging artists before mid-career prices hit

• Secondary Market Masters ($60,000-$100,000): Works by deceased artists with established historical significance

• Curated Collection: 5-8 works forming a serious, cohesive collection worthy of institutional attention

The Reality: You now need advisors: art consultants, appraisers, conservators, framers, insurance specialists, possibly storage. Factor 15-20% of purchase price for these services over time.

FEATURE | *The Price of Admission*

Beginner's Don't:

Don't try to collect everything. Don't buy art purely as investment. Don't trust anyone who guarantees appreciation. Don't skip condition reports, provenance documentation, or proper insurance.

Where to start:

Spend $3,000-$5,000 on a single work from an emerging artist with strong gallery representation (solo show history, positive reviews, clear artistic trajectory). Live with it for six months before buying anything else.

FEATURE | *The Price of Admission*

Classic Cars
The Hidden Costs

At $25,000-$50,000

Entry-level collector cars with genuine appreciation potential.

What's available?

• Japanese Classics ($25,000-$40,000): 1990-97 Mazda MX5 in excellent condition, Toyota Celica GT-Four, Honda Prelude Si

• American Muscle ($30,000-$45,000): Well-restored 1965-66 Mustang coupe (not fastback), Camaro, Chevelle

• European Alternatives ($35,000-$50,000): BMW E30 M3, Porsche 944 Turbo, Mercedes 190E 2.3-16

The Hidden Costs Nobody Mentions:

• Storage: $100-$300/month for climate-controlled (essential)

• Insurance: $500-$1,500/year for agreed-value specialty coverage

• Maintenance: $1,000-$3,000/year even if you barely drive it

• Registration/Fees: $200-$500/year depending on state

• Depreciation During Ownership: Not all classics appreciate

Reality Check: That $35,000 car costs $3,500-$6,000/year to own properly. If you're not driving it regularly, you're funding an expensive sculpture.

At $75,000-$150,000

Serious collector territory with investment-grade potential.

What's available?

• Air-Cooled Porsche ($80,000-$150,000): 911 SC, 964, early 993 in good condition

• Japanese Icons ($100,000-$150,000): Honda NSX, Nissan Skyline GT-R R34 (if legal), Toyota Supra Turbo

• American Muscle Upgrades ($75,000-$120,000): 1969-70 Mustang Boss 302, Chevelle SS 396, Dodge Charger R/T

• European Classics ($90,000-$150,000): Porsche 928 GT, BMW E30 M3 Sport Evolution, Mercedes SL roadsters

Ownership Reality:

• Maintenance: $3,000-$8,000/year for proper care

• Restoration Reserves: Budget $10,000-$20,000 for unexpected issues

• Opportunity Cost: Could this capital appreciate better elsewhere?

Where to focus: Buy the best example you can afford in a single car rather than multiple compromised examples. Condition and provenance matter exponentially more at this level.

At $250,000+

Investment-grade vehicles requiring serious infrastructure.

What's available?

• Supercar Territory ($250,000-$500,000): Ferrari 360/430, Lamborghini Gallardo, early Porsche 911 Turbo (930)

• Blue-Chip Classics ($300,000-$600,000): Porsche 993 GT2, Ferrari 308/328 GTS, Shelby Cobra continuation

• Auction Headliners ($500,000+): Ferrari F40, Porsche 959, significant racing provenance

What You Actually Need:

• Professional Storage Facility: $500-$1,500/month

• Specialist Mechanics: $150-$300/hour labor rates

• Comprehensive Insurance: $3,000-$10,000/year

• Transportation Logistics: $1,500-$5,000 for enclosed transport

• Relationships: Access to the right specialists, restorers, brokers

FEATURE | *The Price of Admission*

Beginner's Don't:

Don't buy a $300,000 car without having owned a $75,000 one first. Don't buy based on auction excitement. Don't assume all classics appreciate. Don't ignore maintenance records or restoration documentation.

Where to start:

A 1990-97 Mazda Miata MX5. Parts available, reliable, appreciating, affordable to maintain, and actually fun to drive. Learn whether you're a collector or an enthusiast before spending $75,000.

FEATURE | *The Price of Admission*

Where to Start
(And What to Avoid)

Smart Entry

For Watches: Start with Tudor, Omega, or Grand Seiko in the $3,000-$7,000 range. Wear it daily for a year. Learn what you value: accuracy, heritage, versatility, complications. Then upgrade strategically.

For Wine: Begin with Bordeaux 2021-2023 vintages at corrected prices. Buy by the case from reputable merchants. Store properly. Drink some, age some. Learn whether you actually enjoy the hobby or just the idea of it.

For Art: Attend galleries monthly for six months before buying anything. When you find an artist whose work you can't stop thinking about, buy a modestly priced work. Live with it. If you still love it after six months, buy more from the same artist or related aesthetic.

For Cars: Buy something you can afford to drive regularly. A $30,000 car you use beats a $150,000 car you visit. Start with Japanese or American classics that have strong parts support and enthusiast communities.

What to Avoid

For Watches:

- Anything bought primarily "as an investment"
- Brands with no service network
- Heavily modified or "custom" pieces
- Purchases from unknown sellers offering deals too good to be true
- Buying purely based on social media hype

For Wine:

- En Primeur purchases (futures) without understanding the market
- Any wine requiring immediate drinking that you're buying "for investment"
- "Trophy" bottles before you've developed your palate
- Buying because a critic gave it 100 points

For Art:

- Any artwork purchased primarily as investment
- Artists with rapidly fluctuating prices and weak institutional support
- Anything requiring you to "learn to like it"
- Purchases based on the artist's Instagram following rather than exhibition history
- Art consultants who won't disclose their commission structure

For Cars:

- Pre-war vehicles (declining values, extremely limited usability)
- Purchases at auction without pre-inspection
- Italian exotics without documented service history
- British sports cars as a first classic (unless you're prepared for electrical hell)

FEATURE | *The Price of Admission*

The Bottom Line

The price of admission isn't just about the purchase price—it's about the total cost of ownership, the learning curve, and the infrastructure required.

A $10,000 watch collection with proper service, insurance, and storage probably costs $12,000 over three years. A $50,000 wine cellar requires $8,000-$12,000 in proper storage and insurance over five years. A $25,000 classic car costs $20,000+ in ownership expenses over five years.

The smartest collectors understand this: Start small, buy quality over quantity, focus on categories that genuinely interest you, build relationships with reputable dealers and galleries, budget 15-25% beyond purchase price for proper ownership, and be prepared to hold for 5-10 years minimum.

The question isn't "How much do I need?" It's "Am I genuinely passionate enough about this to do it properly?"

If the answer is yes, these entry points will get you started. If the answer is "I just think it's a good investment," save your money. The market has no patience for tourists.

What's your entry point? Share your collecting journey at editor@theconnoisseur.com.au

> The question isn't "How much do I need?" It's "Am I genuinely passionate enough about this to do it properly?"

PROFILE | *The Makers*

Master of Light and Shadow
The Luminous Landscapes of Tim Storrier

WORDS | **ROBERT BURATTI**

The Australian art market has produced few artists whose careers demonstrate the sustained institutional support and collector confidence that Tim Storrier has commanded over five decades. While the vagaries of taste have seen many contemporary reputations rise and fall, Storrier's position has remained remarkably stable a trajectory that speaks not merely to fashion but to genuine artistic substance and market acumen.

Born in Sydney in 1949, Storrier entered the professional arena at a propitious moment. The early 1970s saw Australian institutions and collectors beginning to look beyond European modernism toward artists who could articulate a distinctively Australian vision. Storrier's early works, with their haunting depictions of the outback rendered in a vocabulary that married surrealist sensibility with landscape tradition, found immediate resonance. At just nineteen, he became the youngest artist ever to win the Sir John Sulman Prize in 1968, and his first solo exhibition at Australian Galleries in Melbourne in 1969 established a pattern of commercial success that would endure throughout his career.

What distinguishes Storrier's market history is its geographical breadth. While many Australian artists remain primarily collected within their home country, Storrier achieved significant penetration of international markets relatively early in his career. His 1983 solo exhibition at Fischer Fine Art in London proved particularly significant—three works were acquired by the Museum of Modern Art in New York, establishing his presence in one of the world's most important collections. Subsequent exhibitions in Japan, Hong Kong, Singapore, and across Europe established a genuinely global presence. This international dimension has proven crucial to his sustained market strength, insulating his prices from the fluctuations of any single regional economy.

The institutional validation has been equally impressive. The National Gallery of Australia acquired works by Storrier from the outset of his career, with major pieces entering the collection throughout the 1970s and 1980s. Every state gallery in Australia holds significant examples, while the Metropolitan Museum of Art in New York has acquired multiple works—a level of museum representation that places him among Australia's most institutionally collected living artists. His appointment as a Trustee of the Art Gallery of New South Wales in 1989, followed by his award of the Order of Australia in 1994, cemented his position within the cultural establishment.

For collectors, the appeal of Storrier's work operates on multiple levels. Technically, his paintings demonstrate a mastery of traditional painting methods increasingly rare in contemporary practice. His surfaces, built through multiple glazes, possess a luminosity that distinguishes them immediately from works by less accomplished practitioners.

The consistency of his iconography has proven another asset. Storrier's recurring motifs—the burning log, the dramatic sky, the isolated implement—create a coherent body of work easily identifiable yet sufficiently varied to sustain interest. At auction, his major canvases regularly achieve substantial prices, with works reaching well into six figures. His auction record stands at approximately AUD $357,000, achieved in 2013 for "The Fall" at Bonhams Australia—remarkable for a living

PROFILE | *The Makers*

ABOVE: Tim Storrier in the studio with The Speed Dauber, 2023, acrylic on canvas, 183 x 122cm. Photo: Gary Grealy. Courtesy Hopewood House

81

PROFILE | *The Makers*

Australian artist whose primary market remains active.

The 2012 Archibald Prize victory for "The Histrionic Wayfarer (after Bosch)" marked a watershed moment, introducing Storrier to audiences who might not regularly engage with landscape painting. The prize, Australia's most publicised art award, generated significant media coverage and sparked renewed collector interest. Though the win proved controversial—the faceless self-portrait challenged traditional notions of portraiture—it demonstrated Storrier's willingness to push boundaries while maintaining his distinctive visual language. Secondary market prices for earlier works rose appreciably in the following years, while waiting lists for new works extended considerably. This "Archibald effect" demonstrated the ongoing potency of institutional recognition in driving market values.

International collectors have been particularly drawn to Storrier's exploration of the Australian landscape, viewing his works as capturing something essential about the continent's character. European collectors, especially, appreciate the dialogue his work maintains with Romantic landscape traditions—particularly Turner and Friedrich—while transforming them through distinctly Australian subject matter. Japanese collectors have responded to the meditative quality of his compositions and their exploration of impermanence—themes resonant with Eastern aesthetic philosophy. This cross-cultural appeal has proven vital to sustaining international demand.

The market for Storrier divides instructively into distinct periods. Early works from the 1970s, often smaller and more experimental, appeal to collectors interested in artistic development and remain relatively accessible. The major canvases from the 1980s and 1990s—his celebrated "point to point" paintings featuring burning ropes stretched across vast horizons—command premium prices and rarely appear at auction, typically

above: Tim Storrier, *Depot 76 (gone with the wind)* 2025. Acrylic on canvas, 107 x 244 cm. Courtesy Hopewood House

changing hands through private treaty. Works from the "Tickets to Egypt" series of 1986, inspired by his commission from Western Australian businessman Sir Garrick Agnew, represent another highly sought-after period. Recent works benefit from his enhanced reputation post-Archibald while remaining available through his gallery representation.

Unlike artists whose work floods the market during productive periods only to suffer subsequent price corrections, Storrier's output has been judiciously released, maintaining scarcity and supporting price levels. For institutions, Storrier represents a secure acquisition. His work addresses the Australian landscape while demonstrating technical and conceptual sophistication that justifies inclusion in international survey exhibitions. The breadth of scholarly attention his work has received, including major monographs such as Catherine Lumby's "Tim Storrier: The Art of the Outsider" (2000) and Ashley Crawford's "Lines of Fire: Works on Paper by Tim Storrier" (2003), ensures sustained academic interest.

The artist's production extends beyond painting. His prints—lithographs, etchings, and collagraphs—have found strong market

PROFILE | *The Makers*

support, offering entry points for collectors unable to acquire major canvases. More recently, his bronze sculptures have attracted attention, extending his vocabulary into three dimensions while maintaining the iconic imagery that defines his practice. This diversification has broadened his collector base without diluting brand recognition.

Now based in Bowral, New South Wales, Storrier continues working in his mid-seventies with undiminished energy. His recent works demonstrate even greater confidence and economy, paring compositions to their essential elements while maintaining emotional impact. Where younger artists might chase contemporary trends, Storrier has deepened his investigation of longstanding themes—the passage of time, humanity's relationship with landscape, the four elements, and the poetry of decay.

The case for Storrier remains compelling. His age suggests a mature but not concluded career, with major works still entering the market while the historical importance of his contribution becomes increasingly evident. The breadth of institutional holdings ensures sustained scholarly attention, supporting long-term value.

His auction record stands at approximately AUD $357,000 —remarkable for a living Australian artist whose primary market remains active.

Left: Tim Storrier, *A Distance Away - The Nostalgia Of Dusk*, 2018. Acrylic on canvas, 122 x 183cm
Courtesy Hopewood Studio

The international collector base provides market depth unusual for Australian artists. The consistent quality across five decades eliminates concerns about variable periods that plague some artists' markets. Moreover, Storrier's work addresses themes of increasing relevance. Without resorting to didacticism, his paintings evoke the fragility and grandeur of the Australian landscape at a moment of heightened environmental consciousness. The isolated objects in his compositions—often remnants of pastoral or mining activities—suggest both human ambition and its ultimate insignificance against geological time. This prescience ensures his work will resonate with future generations of collectors.

As the Australian art market continues to mature and attract international attention, Storrier's position appears increasingly secure. His sustained excellence, technical mastery, and market discipline have created a body of work that satisfies both aesthetic and investment criteria—the hallmark of genuine collectability. For connoisseurs seeking works by living Australian artists with proven institutional validation, international recognition, and market stability, Storrier represents one of the most rewarding acquisitions available.

Building a Storrier Collection

For collectors considering entry into Storrier's market, strategy depends upon budget and objectives. Works on paper—lithographs, etchings, and collagraphs from editions produced throughout his career—offer accessible entry points, typically ranging from several thousand to twenty thousand Australian dollars. These provide exposure to his iconography and demonstrate his technical command across media. Auction houses regularly offer such works, allowing collectors to study condition and provenance before bidding.

The serious collector seeking investment-grade works should focus on paintings from the 1980s and 1990s, particularly the celebrated "point to point" series featuring burning ropes stretched across horizons. Expect to invest well into six figures for significant canvases from this period. Works from the "Tickets to Egypt" series (1986) command particular premiums given their exhibition history and critical importance to his development.

Primary market prices reflect the artist's enhanced reputation following the 2012 Archibald Prize but offer the advantage of direct provenance and condition guarantees. Patient collectors may secure superior

PROFILE | *The Makers*

Storrier's work addresses themes of increasing relevance. Without resorting to didacticism, his paintings evoke the fragility and grandeur of the Australian landscape at a moment of heightened environmental consciousness.

Left: Tim Storrier, *The Stone Field* 2023 acrylic on canvas 107 x 244 cm. Courtesy Hopewood Studio.

examples by establishing relationships with dealers rather than competing at auction.

When evaluating potential acquisitions, prioritise works with strong exhibition histories, particularly pieces included in major surveys or institutional loans. Documentation matters significantly—original gallery receipts, exhibition labels, and inclusion in published monographs enhance both authenticity and resale value. Condition proves critical given Storrier's glazing techniques; surface abrasions or cleaning damage cannot be easily remedied. Professional conservation assessments should precede any significant purchase.

International collectors face practical considerations. Export permits from Australia may be required for works exceeding certain values, though Storrier's status as a living artist generally facilitates approval. Shipping major canvases requires specialised art transport; insurance valuations should reflect current market rather than historical purchase prices. Currency fluctuations between Australian and other currencies can significantly impact effective purchase prices—advantageous for foreign buyers when the Australian dollar weakens.

For institutional collectors, Storrier offers particular advantages. His work complements holdings of earlier Australian landscape painters while demonstrating contemporary relevance. The technical sophistication satisfies curatorial standards, while the accessible imagery engages public audiences.

Museums lacking representation should consider works spanning multiple decades to demonstrate his stylistic evolution—an early 1970s piece, a major 1980s "point to point" canvas, and a recent meditation on impermanence would constitute an exemplary institutional holding.

The most sophisticated approach combines patience with opportunism. Major Storrier works change hands infrequently; when they do, decisive action proves necessary. Establishing relationships with Australian dealers, monitoring auction previews, and maintaining awareness of private collections coming to market ensures access when opportunities arise.

THE TASTING ROOM

The Art of Not Taking Yourself Too Seriously

Margaret River's Dark Horse Gem

WORDS | JAMES MASTER

Three industry veterans abandon convention to champion Margaret River's overlooked vineyards and the results are anything but goon.

In an industry often paralysed by pretension, Julian Langworthy, John Fogarty, and Mark Fogarty have spent decades playing by the rules. Then they decided to rewrite them. The result? Goon Tycoons—a venture that positions itself somewhere between criminal enterprise and artisan project, "dancing on the verge of stupidity and sensibility."

The premise is deceptively simple: leverage decades of collective expertise to produce small-batch wines from Western Australian vineyards that deserve attention but rarely receive it. Langworthy handles winemaking, John Fogarty manages viticulture, and Mark Fogarty—in their own words—"counts the cash." They describe themselves as being "let out from our everyday jobs to launch our own brand," which suggests either remarkable employers or a midlife crisis executed with unusual precision. Their tagline, "Get Rich, or Drunk Trying," tells you everything you need to know about the operation's seriousness of purpose wedded to fundamental unseriousness of tone.

Natural Is Best, Technique Reigns

Strip away the cheeky nomenclature—Bunch Boy, Hipster Piss, Fiesta De Pantalones—and what emerges is a producer committed to showcasing single-vineyard sites and less familiar varieties through minimalist winemaking. This isn't the natural wine movement's romantic rejection of intervention; it's something more calculated. Technical mastery deployed in service of expressing terroir, not obscuring it.

Consider the 2022 'The Smoking Gun' Chenin Blanc. Sourced from a single Frankland River vineyard, 100% barrel-fermented, the wine presents with pronounced sulphidic reduction—gunsmoke, chipped shell, "unchained minerality" according to the producer. The closing salvo? "If you liked Chenin in the 90's you won't like this." It's a deliberate provocation, acknowledging that this approach to Chenin—flinty, funky, structured—diverges from the fruit-forward, crowd-pleasing style that dominated that decade.

The 2022 'Bunch Boy' Shiraz takes whole-bunch fermentation seriously enough to make it the wine's defining characteristic. Frankland River fruit, handled old-school with manual plunging, delivers concentrated structure and pronounced spice. The description references 1999—a vintage that produced some of Western Australia's finest cool-climate Shiraz—suggesting these aren't winemakers ignorant of history but rather ones choosing to engage with it selectively.

Conditions Demand Adaptation

The 2024 Maradonna Malbec reveals something important about the Goon Tycoons approach: pragmatism. Faced with extreme heat and zero rainfall in both Margaret River and Frankland River, they produced only three wines from the vintage. The Malbec, treated without oak and designed to drink chilled at 15°C, represents intelligent adaptation rather than stubborn adherence to convention. Sometimes the best response to challenging fruit is not to pretend you can make serious, cellar-worthy wine from it—it's to make delicious, immediate wine that serves a different purpose entirely.

Their 2021 Fortified Grenache tells a similar story. When hand-pickers were unavailable and fruit couldn't be selected at peak ripeness, they deployed six-year-old brandy spirit to fortify sweet Grenache from Swinney Vineyard's bush vines.

Two years in barrel later: brandy-soaked Christmas pudding, apricots, raisins.

THE TASTING ROOM

Strip away the cheeky nomenclature and what emerges is a producer committed to showcasing single-vineyard sites through minimalist winemaking.

Above: The Cellar Door of Goon Tycoons, Margaret River, Western Australia.

Two years in barrel later: brandy-soaked Christmas pudding, apricots, raisins. The producer's warning—"This wine will sneak up on you"—is both accurate and necessary.

The Margaret River Anomaly

Goon Tycoons operates in a region famous for Cabernet Sauvignon and Chardonnay, yet their range foregrounds Tempranillo, Fiano, Chenin Blanc, and Teroldego. The 2022 'Prohibition' blends Tempranillo, Shiraz, and Malbec from both Frankland River and Margaret River—a "Twin River" approach that suggests these producers see Western Australia as an integrated region rather than a collection of discrete appellations.

This makes commercial sense when you're working with varieties that don't command Margaret River Cabernet prices. It also reflects genuine conviction that interesting wine doesn't require famous grapes or prestigious postcodes—just good fruit handled intelligently.

Located in Margaret River, the Goon Tycoons cellar door pairs their wines with handcrafted goat and organic cow's milk cheeses from the region. It's open Wednesday through Sunday (daily during summer), suggesting a small operation that hasn't yet scaled to full-time staffing. The cheese focus indicates they understand their wines—structured, acid-driven, often savoury—require food, not just contemplation.

Should You Care?

If you collect First Growth Bordeaux or investment-grade Burgundy, probably not. If you appreciate technically accomplished winemaking applied to unfashionable varieties, absolutely. If you think wine should never take itself too seriously, certainly.

Goon Tycoons represents the sort of mid-career pivot that either produces Australia's most interesting small producers or collapses spectacularly within three vintages. The fact they're making Teroldego and Fiano in Margaret River suggests either hubris or genuine belief these varieties have a future in Western Australia. Time will tell which.

In the meantime, crack open 'The Smoking Gun' and consider whether the Australian wine industry wouldn't benefit from more producers willing to risk looking stupid in pursuit of making something genuinely interesting.

Goon Tycoons Cellar Door

Margaret River, Western Australia
Wednesday–Sunday, 10:00–17:00
goontycoons.com.au

Pick of the Bunch

Five wines that justify the hype—or at least the drive to Margaret River

---

2022 'Bunch Boy' Shiraz
$55
Frankland River

100% whole-bunch fermentation delivers pronounced spice and dense structure from cool-climate fruit. The sort of wine that reminds you why Western Australian Shiraz mattered in the 1990s—then promptly ignores everything that happened since.

2022 'The Smoking Gun' Chenin Blanc
$28
Frankland River, Single Vineyard

Flinty, funky, unapologetically sulphidic. 100% barrel-fermented with pronounced reduction—gunsmoke, oyster shell, relentless minerality. This is Chenin for people who think Chenin has become too polite.

2021 Fortified Grenache
$65
Frankland River, Swinney Vineyard Bush Vines

Goon Tycoons' first foray into fortified wine, born from vintage adversity. Six-year-old brandy spirit fortifies sweet Grenache; two years in barrel produces brandy-soaked Christmas pudding, apricots, dark fruit intensity.

2022 'Prohibition' Twin River Red Blend
$32
Frankland River & Margaret River

Tempranillo, Shiraz, Malbec from two regions behaving as one. Perfumed, savoury lift gives way to juicy, tannin-laden structure. The sort of food-friendly red that handles everything from charcuterie to lamb shoulder.

2024 Maradonna Malbec (Chillable Style)
$32
Margaret River & Frankland River

Vintage conditions from hell—extreme heat, zero rainfall—produced this zero-oak, serve-chilled anomaly. Pure juice, designed for 15°C and summer barbecues. Proof that intelligent winemaking means knowing when not to make "serious" wine.

> ...interesting wine doesn't require famous grapes or prestigious postcodes—just good fruit handled intelligently.

Where to find them:
Goon Tycoons Cellar Door,
Margaret River goontycoons.com.au
Note: Production volumes are small. If you see a bottle, buy it. If you see two, buy both.

THE VIEWING ROOM

Breaking New Ground

Melbourne Art Fair's bold gamble on Design

WORDS | **ROBERT BURATTI**

Asia-Pacific's longest-running contemporary art fair expands its vision with ambitious programming and a groundbreaking 600-square-metre platform for collectable design

The Melbourne Art Fair returns to the Melbourne Convention and Exhibition Centre from 13–16 February 2026, once again establishing itself as the antipodean calendar's most significant contemporary art gathering. For collectors who understand that true acquisition requires more than mere purchasing power, this four-day exhibition offers unparalleled access to museum-quality works and emerging talents destined for institutional recognition.

Situated along the Yarra River in South Wharf, the Melbourne Convention and Exhibition Centre provides the expansive, purpose-built infrastructure essential for presenting contemporary art at scale. The venue's flexible gallery spaces accommodate installations and sculptures that traditional exhibition buildings cannot, whilst maintaining the pristine presentation standards serious collectors expect.

Over 70 carefully curated galleries present works spanning painting, sculpture, photography, video art, and installation, creating a comprehensive survey of contemporary practice that rewards serious engagement. This is not a browsing experience for the casual enthusiast. The Melbourne Art Fair attracts collectors who maintain relationships with galleries across continents, who understand market dynamics, and who recognise that today's emerging artist becomes tomorrow's blue-chip acquisition.

Beyond the Transaction

Whilst the primary gallery floor offers acquisition opportunities, the Fair's true value lies in its programming. The curator-led tours provide scholarly context often absent from commercial gallery visits—essential knowledge for collectors building historically coherent collections rather than merely assembling attractive objects.

The artist talks offer direct dialogue with practitioners, revealing the intellectual frameworks underpinning contemporary practice. These conversations inform collecting decisions in ways that gallery walls and price lists cannot. For those who collect with intent rather than impulse, such access proves invaluable.

The Melbourne Advantage

The Fair's February timing positions it strategically within the international art calendar. Following the December–January northern hemisphere auction season and preceding the March Basel previews, Melbourne offers acquisition opportunities before works enter the secondary market or achieve wider institutional attention. Astute collectors recognise this window.

Melbourne itself enhances the experience. The city's sophisticated dining culture, its architecturally significant hotels, and its genuine appreciation for intellectual discourse create an environment where art fair attendance becomes genuinely pleasurable rather than merely transactional. The MCEC's riverside location—a brief walk from the city's premier restaurants and cultural precinct—allows collectors to experience the Fair without the logistical complications that plague larger international events.

THE VIEWING ROOM

ABOVE: Tove Kjellmark, *The Presence of Her Absence*, 2025. Mixed media, 30 x 40 x 27 cm. Courtesy the artist and Moore Contemporary

THE VIEWING ROOM

The Bottom Line

When: 13–16 February 2026
Where: Melbourne Convention and Exhibition Centre, 1 Convention Centre Place, South Wharf, Melbourne

Opening Hours:

VIP Preview
Thursday, 13 February: 5 – 9pm
General Entry
Friday, 14 February: 11 – 7pm
Saturday, 15 February: 11 – 7pm
Sunday, 16 February: 11 – 5pm

Ticketing:

Standard admission provides gallery floor access. However, serious collectors should consider VIP packages, which include preview access—essential for securing significant works before public viewing—and invitations to the private collectors' reception, where gallery directors and curators offer insights unavailable on the public floor.

Accommodation:

Book early. Melbourne's premier properties fill quickly during the Fair. The Crown Towers, adjacent to the MCEC, offers unmatched convenience for collectors scheduling multiple gallery appointments. The Park Hyatt and InterContinental provide alternative options for those preferring the city centre, though both require brief transfers to South Wharf.

Galleries Not to Miss:

Certain exhibitors warrant priority attention. Roslyn Oxley9, Sydney's venerable contemporary authority, consistently presents museum-calibre works—their booth merits extended viewing regardless of immediate acquisition intent. Melbourne's Niagara Galleries brings four decades of curatorial discernment, whilst Neon Parc offers the city's most intelligent engagement with emerging practice.

MARS Gallery from Melbourne and Perth's Moore Contemporary both maintain programmes sophisticated collectors monitor closely. LON Gallery and Animal House represent Melbourne's increasingly significant

THE VIEWING ROOM

ABOVE LEFT AND RIGHT: Installation view, Melbourne Art Fair 2024. Courtesy Melbourne Art Fair Foundation

contemporary scene with works that reward patient examination.

Art Collective WA offers Perth's distinctive artistic voice—Western Australia's geographic isolation has produced a visual language unlike the eastern seaboard. Finally, Grace (Auckland, Aotearoa) presents New Zealand perspectives essential for collectors building comprehensive Australasian holdings. Serious collectors will schedule appointments with these galleries' directors during preview hours, when conversation occurs without public floor distractions.

Transport:

The MCEC is accessible via the South Wharf tram stop (Route 96, 109, 112) or a pleasant 15-minute walk from Flinders Street Station. Collectors arriving by private car will find dedicated parking facilities, though pre-booking is advisable during Fair dates.

Final Considerations:

The Melbourne Art Fair rewards preparation. Review participating galleries beforehand. Understand which artists interest you and why. Arrive with questions rather than merely chequebook in hand. Serious collecting requires scholarship alongside capital.

For those who approach art acquisition as an intellectual pursuit rather than decorative shopping, the Melbourne Art Fair offers four days of genuine discovery. It remains Australia's most significant opportunity to engage with contemporary practice at the highest level—provided one arrives prepared to look, learn, and then perhaps acquire.

> The Melbourne Art Fair rewards preparation. Review participating galleries beforehand. Understand which artists interest you and why.

THE GRAND TOUR | *Travel*

Concrete Ambitions
Brutalism's Unlikely Luxury Masterpiece

WORDS | **ROBERT BURATTI**

Perth has never quite known what to do with its brutalist buildings. The city's 1960s architectural inheritance—those hulking concrete monoliths that sprang up during the mining boom—remains largely misunderstood, occasionally reviled, and frequently demolished. Which makes The Duxton Hotel an intriguing anomaly: a former Australian Taxation Office building that's somehow managed to become one of Perth's most compelling five-star addresses.

THE GRAND TOUR | *Travel*

THE GRAND TOUR | *Travel*

In a city now dominated by glossy international brands—the Ritz-Carlton on Elizabeth Quay, COMO The Treasury in its heritage digs, Crown Towers with its casino-resort ambitions—The Duxton has carved out a different position entirely. No global chain playbook. No desperate attempts to mimic somewhere else. Just a sixteen-storey tower at 1 St Georges Terrace that wears its 1962 brutalist bones unapologetically and has, through careful stewardship, transformed into Perth's leading independent luxury hotel.

This was never meant to be beautiful. Built for bureaucrats, not bon vivants, the structure embodies what architectural historian Robert Cook calls Perth's "reserved" approach to brutalism—less aggressive than its international cousins, but still fundamentally uncompromising. The transformation to hotel in 1996, and the recent $2 million renovation completed in 2024, haven't tried to apologise for the architecture. They've simply worked with it. And in doing so, they've created something increasingly rare: a luxury hotel with genuine character.

Location Location

If the Ritz-Carlton has Elizabeth Quay's waterfront glamour and Crown Towers has its resort sprawl, The Duxton has something more fundamental: proper city centrality. The address delivers Perth Concert Hall next door, the Swan River a genuine five-minute walk (not hotel marketing five minutes—actual five minutes), Elizabeth Quay's waterfront close enough to access without effort.

More crucially, it occupies the genuine business and cultural heart of Perth's CBD. St. George's Anglican Cathedral, The Perth Mint, and the city's key business districts radiate outward from this point. When diplomats and corporate decision-makers choose The Duxton, they're not making a lifestyle statement—they're making a practical calculation about where power and culture intersect in Perth. That's why the hotel consistently attracts dignitaries, senior executives, and the sort of travellers who care more about substance than Instagram moments.

THE GRAND TOUR | *Travel*

ABOVE: Poolside cocktails. Courtesy The Duxton Hotel Perth

In a city now dominated by glossy international brands, The Duxton has carved out a different position entirely. No global chain playbook. No desperate attempts to mimic somewhere else.

Hay Street Mall sits within easy walking distance for those requiring retail access. Kings Park's 400 hectares of bushland and botanical gardens lie just beyond the CBD's western edge. But the real advantage is this: you can conduct serious business, access Perth's limited but improving cultural institutions, and be back in your room within minutes. In a city this spread out, that matters more than most visitors initially realise.

Rooms with Genuine Space

Here's where The Duxton's brutalist origins deliver unexpected dividends. The 304 rooms and suites—ranging from well-conceived deluxe configurations to the recently expanded Presidential Suite—benefit from the building's original design in ways that contemporary construction rarely achieves. Brutalist architecture, for all its aesthetic controversies, tends toward genuinely generous proportions. No developer trying to maximise room count per floor. No creative accounting with "usable space."

The result: bathrooms with actual room to move. Many feature separate full-size baths and walk-in showers that don't require Sophie's choice between washing your hair and bruising your elbows. The contemporary design doesn't try too hard—neutral palettes, quality materials, furnishings that look expensive because they are rather than because they're trying to appear expensive. Swan River views dominate from the better rooms, particularly the newly refurbished Club Rooms on the upper floors. Floor-to-ceiling windows take advantage of Perth's exceptional light without the aggressive floor-to-ceiling glass curtains that plague newer hotels (and their resulting climate control nightmares). The 100+ Mbps WiFi actually functions as advertised—a detail worth noting in an era when five-star hotels routinely struggle to provide connectivity that matches a decent apartment.

Twenty-four-hour room service remains genuinely available. Not "limited menu after 10pm" room service. Actual room service. For

> Brutalist architecture, for all its aesthetic controversies, tends toward genuinely generous proportions. No developer trying to maximise room count per floor.

business travellers on international schedules or those who simply prefer dining privately, this represents luxury as utility rather than theatre.

Yes, there's a pillow menu. Whether this represents genuine luxury or the hospitality industry's collective inability to simply provide decent pillows is open to interpretation. But the beds themselves—actually comfortable, properly firm without being punishing—suggest someone in procurement understands the difference between luxury and luxury signalling. The recent $2 million renovation focused intelligently on areas that matter: Club Rooms that feel genuinely premium rather than simply redecorated, the Presidential Suite expanded to actually accommodate presidential schedules, and infrastructure upgrades that position the hotel for another decade rather than requiring constant patchwork maintenance. This is patient capital at work, not quarterly earnings optimisation.

Dining with Purpose

Firewater Grille stakes its reputation on steak, which could be dismissed as the reliable refuge of hotel dining rooms everywhere—except when executed properly. The restaurant's focus on Western Australian wine regions provides genuine discovery opportunities for visitors unfamiliar with

THE GRAND TOUR | *Travel*

ABOVE: One of the great offerings at the Duxton Hotel Bar. OPPOSITE: The stunning renovated lobby. Courtesy The Duxton Hotel Perth

Margaret River, Swan Valley, and the Great Southern's increasingly impressive offerings. This isn't token local sourcing; it's a wine list that demonstrates why Perth's geographic isolation has forced local producers to achieve genuine quality.

The "modern international cuisine" descriptor—usually code for "nothing too challenging"—here translates more charitably to a menu that respects ingredients without unnecessary complication. The kitchen's recent revitalization as part of the hotel's renovation has brought in culinary programming that engages with Perth's increasingly multicultural food culture rather than simply defaulting to steakhouse conservatism. The refurbished Lobby Bar succeeds where many hotel bars fail: it's somewhere you might actually choose to drink rather than simply tolerate. The terrace views, the surprisingly competent fish and chips that have returning guests ordering them twice, the general absence of aggressive "mixology" that plagues contemporary hotel bars—it suggests management understands the difference between a hotel bar and a bar that happens to be in a hotel.

The Swan River Lounge, reserved for adult guests, provides the sort of quiet, refined space that's increasingly difficult to find in hotels chasing the "vibrant" and "energetic" aesthetics that make peaceful conversation impossible. For business meetings that require discretion or simply unwinding with something decent to read, it's the sort of amenity that reminds you why hotels used to be sanctuaries from rather than amplifiers of urban energy.

The Independent Advantage

Operating independently from major hotel groups means The Duxton can't fall back on the algorithmic consistency that characterises chain hospitality. This cuts both ways, certainly—service depends more heavily on individual staff members rather than corporate training modules. But the 8.8 overall rating and particularly strong 9.3 for location suggest a property that has found its equilibrium. What independence actually delivers: flexibility to make decisions based on guest needs rather than brand standards written in distant headquarters. The recent partnership exclusively with Western Australian suppliers for the renovation—Real Eyes Design, Atifax Project Solutions, Cottesloe furniture maker Bethany James, and various local contractors—represents the sort of decision that wouldn't survive a corporate procurement process. It's more expensive. It's more complicated. It's also the reason the hotel's refurbishment feels genuinely connected to place rather than imported from a global design playbook.

Staff consistency matters more here than at chain properties, and reviews suggest The Duxton has largely solved this equation. From valet parking through concierge services to restaurant staff, the operation demonstrates what happens when a hotel culture is built rather than imposed. The service philosophy appears to be "anticipate intelligently" rather than "execute the script." For travellers who've endured one too many over-rehearsed hotel interactions, this represents meaningful differentiation.

For Perth's limited but growing community of collectors, business owners, and travellers

THE GRAND TOUR | *Travel*

who value substance over brand recognition, The Duxton's independence reads as confidence rather than isolation. It's a hotel that knows what it is and has no interest in being mistaken for somewhere else.

The Brutalist Paradox

Here's what makes The Duxton interesting: it hasn't tried to hide its architectural origins. While Perth has spent decades either ignoring or demolishing its brutalist legacy, this building has leaned into the aesthetic. The result is a hotel with actual character—which in the homogenised world of contemporary luxury hospitality, might be the rarest amenity of all. The outdoor pool, fitness center, and sauna deliver the expected amenities without particular distinction. But in a city where architectural memory is short and the impulse to "refresh" often means obliterate, The Duxton stands as evidence that Perth's brutalist buildings might have more potential than we've given them credit for. Not every conversion needs to apologise for what came before.

Perth's luxury hotel scene divides into predictable camps. The Ritz-Carlton delivers the global brand's reliable formula—impeccable on paper, occasionally soulless in practice. COMO The Treasury offers heritage-building romance for those who find 19th-century State Buildings more palatable than 1960s concrete.

Crown Towers provides resort-scale excess for visitors who want every amenity catalogued and available, even if they'll never use most of them. The Duxton occupies different territory entirely. It's where diplomats stay when they're in Perth for work rather than performance. Where senior executives choose to sleep because location and efficiency matter more than lobby theatre. Where return visitors accumulate because the hotel has figured out that genuine luxury means removing friction rather than adding spectacle.

In a city of just over two million that still feels like it's deciding what it wants to be when it grows up, The Duxton has the confidence to already know its answer. It's Perth's best luxury hotel for people who actually live in the world rather than simply passing through it for social media documentation.

The 9.3 location score tells part of the story. The 8.8 overall rating—exceptional for independent properties competing against corporate hospitality machines—tells another. But the real metric is simpler: it's the hotel where informed travellers return, where business gets conducted efficiently, and where Perth's actual power structure convenes when the setting needs to match the seriousness of the conversation. Not the most expensive option in Perth. Not the one with the splashiest marketing campaign. Simply the one that delivers luxury as reliability, consistency, and genuine understanding of what discerning travellers actually require. In an era of hospitality excess, that restraint reads as remarkable sophistication.

The Duxton Hotel Perth
1 St Georges Terrace
Perth CBD, Western Australia 6000
perth.duxtonhotels.com

THE GRAND TOUR | *Travel*

In a city still defining its identity, here's a property that's already decided: substance over spectacle, location over performance, and architectural honesty over apologetic renovation. For travellers who've stayed everywhere else and found it all somewhat predictable, The Duxton offers something increasingly rare—a luxury hotel with actual point of view.

LEFT: Expansive interiors of the Club Room King Riverview.
RIGHT: The Swan River Lounge. Courtesy The Duxton

COLLECTOR CLASSIC

Collector Classic
The Art of Collecting Vintage Omega

WORDS | ROBERT BURATTI

For the discerning horological collector, vintage Omega timepieces represent an exceptional intersection of Swiss craftsmanship, historical significance, and accessible luxury. Whilst the marque's Speedmaster Professional—the "Moonwatch"—commands most of the spotlight, serious collectors understand that Omega's vintage catalogue extends far deeper, particularly amongst the Genève, De Ville, and Seamaster collections. Each line possesses distinct characteristics, collector appeal, and market dynamics that warrant careful consideration.

COLLECTOR CLASSIC

Images courtesy of Steel City Watches and OMEGA.

Genève: The Elegant Workhorse

Introduced in 1960, the Omega Genève was positioned as the brand's entry-level dress watch, yet this designation belies the quality and appeal these timepieces hold for today's collectors. The Genève was produced in numerous variations over its three-decade production run, featuring both manual-wind and automatic movements.

Collector Appeal: The Genève›s charm lies in its honest simplicity. These watches eschew complications and sporting pretensions in favour of clean, elegant design. Cases range from 33mm to 36mm—perfectly proportioned for vintage dress watches—and dials frequently showcase Omega›s mastery of applied indices and dauphine hands.

Value Proposition: Genève models represent the most accessible entry point into vintage Omega collecting. Well-preserved examples with original dials typically range from $1,500 to $4,500, depending on movement (calibres 601, 613, and 1012 being most common), case condition, and dial configuration. Rare dial variants—particularly those with intricate guilloché patterns or unusual colour combinations—can command premiums of 50-100% above standard models.

What to Seek: Original dials are paramount. The Genève line has been plagued by replacement dials and refinishing. Examine printing quality closely; factory dials display crisp, evenly applied text with proper font characteristics. The Omega logo should be precisely rendered, and any applied indices should be securely fastened with no evidence of adhesive. Service history is valuable, but unserviced watches with original movements often present better long-term value than those with replacement parts.

De Ville: Sophistication Refined

The De Ville ("of the city" in French) emerged in 1960 as a sub-line of the Seamaster collection before achieving independent status in 1967. These watches embodied urban sophistication, offering slimmer profiles, more refined finishing, and often incorporating design elements reflecting contemporary architectural and artistic movements.

Collector Appeal: De Ville watches from the 1960s and 1970s represent Omega at its most design-forward. The collection embraced both conservatively elegant dress watches and boldly styled pieces that captured the era›s aesthetic adventurousness. Particularly collectible are examples with integrated bracelets, sector dials, or unconventional case shapes—hooded lugs, tonneau cases, and cushion forms all appear throughout the range.

Value Proposition: De Ville values vary considerably based on style and rarity. Conservative dress models with time-only complications typically sell for $2,200 to $6,500. However, distinctive examples—particularly those with original integrated bracelets or featuring popular movements like the automatic calibre 1012 or chronograph

COLLECTOR CLASSIC

The vintage Omega market rewards patience, research, and discernment—offering extraordinary diversity from accessible dress watches to significant historical pieces.

COLLECTOR CLASSIC

> Whilst Speedmaster Professional models receive the most attention, the Genève, De Ville, and Seamaster collections offer superior value propositions for knowledgeable collectors.

calibre 321—can achieve $9,000 to $27,000 or beyond. The De Ville Chronograph models from the late 1960s and early 1970s have experienced particular appreciation, with examples powered by the calibre 321 or 861 attracting serious collector interest.

What to Seek: For De Ville pieces, originality extends beyond the dial to include bracelets, which were often integral to the design. A De Ville with its original integrated bracelet in good condition can be worth double that of the watch head alone. Examine case finishing carefully; De Ville watches often featured brushed and polished surfaces, and amateur polishing has destroyed countless examples. The presence of crisp bevels and defined angles indicates sympathetic handling.

Seamaster: Versatile Icon

The Seamaster line, inaugurated in 1948, represents Omega's longest-running collection. Whilst modern Seamaster Professional dive watches dominate contemporary awareness, vintage Seamasters encompass an extraordinarily diverse range of styles, from elegant dress pieces to robust tool watches.

Collector Appeal: The vintage Seamaster's appeal derives from its versatility and the collection's historical depth. Early Seamasters (1940s-1950s) feature classically proportioned cases, applied gold indices, and exquisite dial finishing. The 1960s introduced sportier variants, culminating in the Seamaster 300—Omega's professional dive watch—and various chronograph models. By the 1970s, the line had expanded to include everything from ultra-thin dress pieces to robust dive instruments.

Value Proposition: Seamaster values span the widest range of any Omega collection. Standard three-hand Seamasters from the 1950s-1970s typically trade between $1,800 and $7,500, depending on condition and movement quality. However, specific references command substantially higher prices:

Seamaster 300 (Ref. 165.024 and earlier): $15,000-$45,000+, with first-generation references from the 1950s exceeding $75,000 in exceptional condition.

Seamaster Chronographs: Models featuring the calibre 321 or 861 movements range from

COLLECTOR CLASSIC

> Original dials are paramount. The Genève line has been plagued by replacement dials and refinishing—examine printing quality closely.

$9,000 to $37,000+, with rare dial variants commanding premiums.

Seamaster De Ville Chronographs: These hybrid pieces, produced before the De Ville achieved independent status, are increasingly sought after, trading between $7,500 and $22,000.

What to Seek: For Seamaster collecting, the movement matters immensely. The calibre 321 (shared with the Speedmaster) represents the pinnacle, whilst calibres 561, 562, and 564 offer excellent quality at lower price points. Dive watch variants require particular scrutiny: examine cases for corrosion, ensure crowns are original (or period-correct), and verify that any replacement parts are appropriate to the reference. Luminous material on vintage dive watches should show consistent ageing across hands and dial markers—mismatched patina often indicates replacement parts.

Building a Cohesive Collection

For collectors seeking to build a meaningful vintage Omega collection, consider a thematic approach:

The Movement Collector: Focus on acquiring examples of Omega's finest calibres—the 321, 561, 564, and 1012. This approach prioritises horological merit over model designation.

The Design Historian: Collect pieces that represent distinct aesthetic periods—1950s elegance, 1960s modernism, 1970s boldness. This permits exploration of Omega's design evolution whilst maintaining collection coherence.

The Specialist: Deep-dive into a single line—Seamaster 300s, De Ville Chronographs, or Genève dress watches—acquiring variations that demonstrate the range within that collection.

Authentication and Condition

Regardless of model, certain principles apply to vintage Omega collecting:

Movement Authenticity: Omega movements should display appropriate calibre markings, finishing quality, and serial numbers consistent with the case. Examine escapement components and balance wheel for signs of quality—these are difficult to counterfeit convincingly.

Dial Integrity: Original Omega dials exhibit superb printing quality, with even ink distribution and crisp edges. Beware of refinished dials, which, whilst sometimes well-executed, diminish collector value by 40-60%.

Case Condition: Moderate wear is acceptable and often preferable to over-polishing. Original case proportions—particularly lug thickness and bezel edges—indicate sympathetic ownership.

Service History: Documented service history

COLLECTOR CLASSIC

adds value, but only if performed by qualified watchmakers using appropriate replacement parts. Amateur servicing or incorrect parts devalue pieces substantially.

The Bottom Line

The vintage Omega market has matured considerably over the past decade. Whilst Speedmaster Professional models receive the most attention, the Genève, De Ville, and Seamaster collections offer superior value propositions for knowledgeable collectors.

Genève watches, undervalued relative to their quality, present particular opportunities. Well-preserved examples with original dials and appropriate patina offer an accessible entry point with potential for appreciation as collectors increasingly recognise the line's merits.

De Ville chronographs and distinctive dress pieces from the 1960s-1970s have experienced steady appreciation, driven by growing interest in mid-century design and these models' relative scarcity compared to Speedmasters.

Seamaster 300s and chronographs have appreciated substantially, approaching—and in some cases exceeding—Speedmaster Professional values. However, standard Seamaster dress watches remain undervalued, offering discerning collectors an opportunity to acquire exceptional timepieces at reasonable prices.

Collecting vintage Omega watches—particularly amongst the Genève, De Ville, and Seamaster lines—rewards patience, research, and discernment. These collections offer extraordinary diversity, from accessible dress watches to significant historical pieces, enabling collectors to engage with Swiss horology's finest traditions without the premiums commanded by Rolex or Patek Philippe. The most successful collectors prioritise originality, condition, and personal aesthetic satisfaction over short-term market dynamics. Whether drawn to the honest elegance of a Genève, the sophisticated styling of a De Ville, or the versatile appeal of a Seamaster, vintage Omega watches offer compelling opportunities for those willing to develop expertise and exercise patience in their pursuit.

> De Ville chronographs and distinctive dress pieces from the 1960s-1970s have experienced steady appreciation, driven by growing interest in mid-century design.

The Hunt
Six Objects of Desire for the Discerning Collector

SUMMER-AUTUMN | 2026

The Hunt is your biannual guide to the acquisitions that matter. We don't feature what's readily available—only the objects worth pursuing with determination, patience, and proper expertise.

1 Patek Philippe Nautilus Ref. 5711 Tiffany Blue Dial

The holy grail for serious collectors. With production ceased in 2021, the Tiffany-stamped variant has become impossibly rare. Expect to navigate grey market premiums of 300-400% over retail, but for those who understand horological significance, this represents the intersection of two iconic brands at a pivotal moment in watchmaking history. Authentication is critical—seek provenance documentation and consider independent verification.

TIFFANY & CO.

THE HUNT

2 1973 Porsche 911 Carrera RS 2.7 Lightweight

The purist's 911. With only 200 lightweight versions produced, finding an unmolested example with matching numbers and original paint has become increasingly challenging. The Australian market sees perhaps one or two annually. Values have appreciated 400% in the past decade, but more importantly, this represents driving pleasure that modern engineering simply cannot replicate. Look for comprehensive service history and pre-purchase inspection by marque specialists.

Image courtesy of Sothebys

THE HUNT

3 1990 Domaine de la Romanée-Conti, La Tâche

Whilst DRC's Romanée-Conti commands headlines, La Tâche from this exceptional vintage offers profound complexity at a marginally more accessible entry point. The 1990 vintage is reaching its peak drinking window, making acquisition urgent for those seeking immediate gratification rather than further cellaring. Provenance and storage history are paramount—reject anything without impeccable documentation. Expect $6,500-9,500 per bottle from reputable sources.

4 Hermès Birkin 25 in Bleu Nuit Togo with Palladium Hardware

The compact Birkin 25 has emerged as the connoisseur's choice—more refined than the ubiquitous 30, more practical than the diminutive Kelly. Bleu Nuit represents Hermès' colour mastery: sophisticated navy that transcends trends. Building a relationship with your local boutique remains the only legitimate path to acquisition. Grey market premiums have become absurd; patience and cultivation of boutique relationships will be rewarded.

THE HUNT

6 Paintings by Gaypalani Wanambi

Above: Gaypalani Wanambi, Burwu, Blosssom, 2025. Image courtesy of Museum & Art Gallery of Northern Territory, Darwin.

The 2025 winner of the National Aboriginal & Torres Srait Islander Art Awards (NATSIAA) represents the intersection of ancestral knowledge and radical material innovation that sophisticated collectors recognise as genuinely significant. Working from Buku-Larrnggay Mulka Art Centre in Yirrkala, Wanambi transforms salvaged road signs and industrial scrap metal into intricate engravings depicting her Marrakulu clan's songlines. As the leading female practitioner of the Found movement—which her late father pioneered—she's creating work that international institutions are only beginning to understand. Her recent NATSIAA triumph will accelerate market recognition; astute collectors should acquire now, directly through Buku-Larrnggay Mulka. Expect $15,000-145,000 for significant works, with major pieces commanding more.

THE HUNT

5 Aman's Inaugural Through-Journey: Japan

Aman has pioneered a new category: the through-journey connecting three of their Japanese properties via private experiences most travellers will never access. Limited to 12 departures annually, the 14-day itinerary spans Kyoto's temples, Tokyo's modern energy, and mountain hot springs. This represents experiential luxury at its zenith—not merely accommodation, but transformative immersion. Bookings open 18 months in advance; expect $95,000-125,000 per couple.

FINAL THOUGHT

Final Thought
On the Art of Keeping Time

WORDS | **ROBERT BURATTI**

There's a particular satisfaction in winding a mechanical watch each morning. Not because it's necessary—quartz keeps better time, and your phone is always in your pocket—but because the ritual matters.

The connoisseur understands this instinctively. Whether it's decanting a wine that doesn't strictly need it, polishing shoes that already shine, or taking the longer route home in a car that begs to be driven, these small ceremonies separate living well from merely getting by.

In an age obsessed with efficiency, we've become suspicious of anything that demands our time without obvious return. But perhaps that's precisely the point. The things worth collecting, worth cherishing, worth pursuing—they're rarely the most convenient option.

They're the ones that make you pause.

The next time someone asks why you bother with vintage watches when your phone tells time, or why you collect first editions when digital is easier, or why you travel to vineyards when wine shops deliver—smile, and say nothing.

Some things are better experienced than explained.

The Connoisseur returns in six months. Until then, wind your watches, drive your cars, and drink the good bottles. Life's too short to save everything for later.

www.ingramcontent.com/pod-product-compliance
Lightning Source LLC
Chambersburg PA
CBHW040059160426
43193CB00002B/20